The Catalyst

The Catalyst

RUDOLF VON LEYDEN and India's Artistic Awakening

Reema Desai Gehi

SPEAKING TIGER

SPEAKING TIGER BOOKS LLP
125A, Ground Floor, Shahpur Jat, near Asiad Village,
New Delhi 110049

First published in hardback by Speaking Tiger Books 2024

Photographs: All images except where specified courtesy James von Leyden and Flora Veit-Wild from the Leyden Family Archives, the U.K and Germany.

ISBN: 978-93-5447-795-9
eISBN: 978-93-5447-820-8

The publishing of the book has been supported by
German Federal Foreign Office and The Raza Foundation

Book design: Rishita Chandra
Typeset in Galliard by Bharati Khule
Printed at Thompson Press, Delhi

With thinker's frown the wrinkled brow
harbours but thought elect,
the tired head seeks rest, and how the
scalp receding heightens the effect.

Not cast in bronze, claiming cerulean fame,
not cast in stone posterity to master —
his friends themselves will hesitate to name
the thing revealed. It's only clay and plaster.

- R.v. L

Head by S.K.Bakre

Contents

FOREWORD BY KRISHEN KHANNA

When I was asked to write a foreward to this book on Rudi, I thought of the obituary I had written on his death. Quite without thinking I wrote it as if he was alive. How could a man like Rudie just cease to exist. And now while writing on his actions and his legacy I find myself almost as if he was sitting beside me. He belonged to a generation of immortals. It amazes me to think that he and almost all of the artists he wrote about have gone. The values they cherished in art are still there and the works of those artists are still acclaimed and are considered relevant. It was one of periods which produced several artists of distinction and Rudi acted as an active agent. He was a person with a great perception and when confronted with situations in art which he couldnt quite understand, he listened with intent & got into long arguments, mulled over propositions he didn't fully comprehend and when necessary, he modified his views. More often than not his views prevailed & long arguments ended in a confirmation of his opinions. He never said as much but he was still a votery of Beauty and was not given over to tightly held theories, there was much open mindedness which made discussions more lively. As was to be expected, his abilities + his very imposing presence, also generated a kind of criticism held by some who considered that he was violating Indian sensibilities and planting foreign views and aesthetic theories which were inimical to what was considered as specifically Indian. These insular views could not accomodate Rudi's knowledge of Indian aesthetics which he propounded quite frequently. But more than talking theory, one had only to look at the collections he made of Indian Sculpture & paintings and more especially of Gangifa, that complex mixture of art and gaming. I myself thought this pasion was somewhat frivolous until I heard him lecture on this subject at India International Centre. I was astonished at the complexity of this "sport". There were so many sides to his character which might easily make me go on and on, much like long evenings with him which seemed endless. I have not said a word about the effects which his presence created. They are there to be realised by those who are interested. Great ideas are immutable and can exist without those who generated them.

Krishen Khanna

PREFACE

The sky turned an ominous dark grey as Mumbai witnessed a dramatic downpour on 23 July 2016. It was as if the portentous skies were mourning along with the Indian art world, which had lost one of its master painters, Sayed Haider Raza.

Raza's demise in Delhi officially marked the end of an era. At 94, Raza was the last surviving founding member of the Bombay Progressive Artists' Group (PAG), arguably the most important art movement in modern India. As a 25-year-old artist, Raza together with his fellow contemporaries—an audacious 24-year-old Francis Newton Souza, who was rusticated from Sir J.J. School of Art for participating in the 1942 Quit India Movement, and a mild-mannered self-taught painter, 33-year-old Krishnaji Howlaji Ara—convened on the eve of India's independence to form the PAG in 1947. Each member inducted one artist: Ara brought in painter and sculptor Sadanand Bakre, Raza invited Hari Ambadas Gade, and Souza secured the iconoclastic Maqbool Fida Husain, a former billboard painter. At age 31, Husain had recently quit his job at a furniture store in Churchgate, Bombay, signifying his own freedom from full-time employment, a proclamation that coincided with India's independence.

The PAG vocally dismissed the past. They rejected the British academic style of painting that was taught at the Sir J.J. School of Art, and they found no connection with the Bengal School, which seemed irrelevant to the realities of their time.

Bombay was the fulcrum for PAG's activities.

Rudolf von Leyden at The Times of India

At the close of the 1940s, the city was perched on the cusp of change. The British were about to relinquish their colonial hold, signalling the end of an era that had profoundly shaped the city's identity. The impending independence of India was set to transform the city's social, cultural and economic landscape.

As PAG navigated a political landscape characterised by the dual sentiments of the joy of independence and the anguish of Partition, a German art critic, Rudolf von Leyden, popularly known as Rudi, emerged as an influential but often overlooked figure in Bombay's post-independence art scene. As a refugee from Nazi Germany, he found himself enchanted by the vibrancy of India's avant-garde artists and committed himself to elevating their work through his astute criticism and advocacy.

The country aspired to rebuild; the responsibility of crafting the narrative for a 'new India' fell on the cultural community: writers, poets, filmmakers and artists. 'The exuberance of being the first

The PAG members and friends

courtesy of DAG Archives

generation of independent India created a new wave. It was when the fine arts, music and theatre blossomed, and I found myself caught in it,' reflected theatre veteran Vijaya Mehta.[1]

In many senses, the group conformed to this concept of a 'new India,' and, owing to the religious and caste diversity within their ranks—not by design but by coincidence—they even embodied the Nehruvian philosophy of a secular India.

Nonetheless, PAG's co-founder Souza, often considered the *enfant terrible* of the Indian art world, infamous for his provocative statements, ascribed the group's formation to dissatisfaction with the trite local art system and a fervent desire to challenge it.

In a piercing article titled, 'Progressive Artists' Group' for the *Patriot* magazine in 1984, Souza wrote:

> I had begun to notice the J.J. School of Art turned out an awful number of bad artists year after year and the Bombay Art Society showed awful crap in its Annual Exhibitions, which comprised the amateur efforts of

> some memsahibs in India who were pampered by British imperialism. Hence, this pretty-pretty painting together with the work of several artists coming out of the art school exhibited once a year in the Annual Exhibition had no direction, no goal, no inspiration, no energy—regardless of the style or method they chose to work in. It then occurred to me to form a group to give ourselves an incentive.

In keeping with this spirit, the group, whose initial meetings were held in the office of the Friends of Soviet Union at Girgaum in Bombay, had its first solo show in 1949 in Baroda. Subsequently, they showed their work at the Bombay Art Society Salon.

Mulk Raj Anand, the erstwhile editor of the renowned magazine *Marg* and a pioneer of Indo-Anglian fiction, author of the ground-breaking book, *Untouchable* (1935), inaugurated the show. It earned a review by one of the group's biggest champions, Rudi, the art critic of *The Times of India*. He wrote:

> The six artists, Ara, sculptor Bakre, Gade, Husain, Raza, and Souza have formed a distinct group despite their very different artistic approaches and tempers. They are not satisfied with the ready-made conventions either of the academic western nor of the academic traditional school. In the words of Samuel Butler[2], which they have set as a motto over this exhibition, "young art must be working out its own salvation from efforts in all fear and trembling." It can also not be said that they have simply exchanged the conventions of the old schools for the obscure code of modern painting. Those who have followed the work of these artists over the past years will know of the struggle, the experiments, the trials that lie behind the considerable achievement which this exhibition represents.[3]

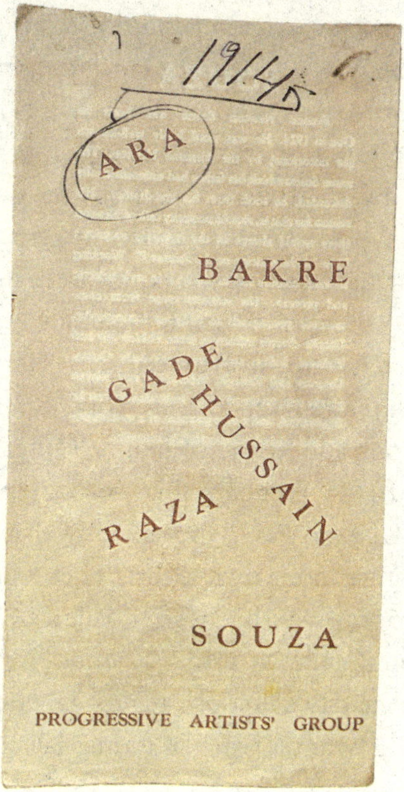

The PAG's Bombay show brochure

For the Bombay Progressives, it was never about flaunting their individual identities. Artist Krishen Khanna stated, 'An artist mattered least; his personality came in last. What mattered was his vision, which should predominate.'

Though the group never formally disbanded, after their exhibitions in Baroda and Bombay, Souza and Bakre left for London in 1949 and 1951 respectively, while Raza went to study at the *École Nationale Supérieure des Beaux-Arts* (ENSB-A) in Paris on a French government scholarship in 1950. The remaining members endeavoured to sustain the group, inviting Vasudeo Gaitonde, A.A. Raiba, Hazarnis, Bhanu Athaiya (née Rajopadhye), Mohan Samant, and Krishen Khanna to exhibit alongside them in 1953.

During this phase, the artistic evolution of the PAG members was evident. The highly celebrated Gaitonde, who was affiliated with the Progressive Artists' Group for only a brief period, began transitioning from figurative art to non-objective art. A. A. Raiba's work was marked by bold shapes and strong outlines, Hazarnis found his niche in post-impressionistic snowscapes, and Bhanu adeptly painted but ultimately pursued a career in costume design for films. An early modernist painter Samant—a lifelong player of the Indian bowed string instrument, the sarangi—took off to Italy on a scholarship and later to New York. Briefly, he joined the Bombay Group, alongside Krishen Khanna. Other notable artists in the group included K.K. Hebbar, Shiavax Chavda, D.G. Kulkarni, Harkrishnan Lall, Laxman Pai, Baburao Sadwelkar, Ara and Gade[4], each an eminent figure in his own right. 'They were all much older in age than the Progressives, but were goaded by their enthusiasm and ambition,' noted gallerist Dadiba Pundole, whose father Kali established one of the city's first private art galleries in 1963, at the behest of Rodabeh Sawhney, sister of industrialist J.R.D Tata.

✣

The PAG's zeal also made an impact at the Sir J.J. School of Art, referred to as J.J., where most of the institute's graduates conformed to the group's ideology. J.D. Gondhalekar, appointed as dean at J.J. in 1953, had a reputation for being a nonconformist. He brought a much-needed change in the traditional pedagogy, a programme largely inspired by the Bauhaus movement[5] that began in Germany before the Second World War. Unlike his predecessors, Gondhalekar encouraged students to visit different departments and promoted the sharing of ideas and philosophies within the campus.

Artist Akbar Padamsee saw Gondhalekar as a likely ally who would come to his defence in court when he was charged with obscenity in 1954. 'Though he was sympathetic towards my case, he categorically told me that since he was a government servant, he couldn't appear against the very system he works for,' Padamsee remembered, when we met at his studio in Prabhadevi, Mumbai, in 2017.

The studio, bathed in ample light, was dotted with his recent colourful metascapes and portraits. Padamsee took a break from painting as he narrated his side of the case with the excitement of a child at the age of 89. I had to strain my ears to follow Padamsee's frail voice as he recounted the controversial court case.

On 29 April 1954, Padamsee opened his exhibition at the landmark Jehangir Art Gallery—one of the early public art spaces in Bombay—with considerable fanfare, attended by his friends, family and well-wishers.

The next day, a suspicious-looking man approached Padamsee and asked, 'Do you have any photographs on sale?'

Padamsee, glancing around at his landscapes and portraits, replied, 'If any of these images interest you, you could have them.'

The gentleman winced. 'I mean those kinds of photographs,' he said, while slyly gesturing towards two paintings—*Lovers 1* and *Lovers 2*. Both depicted a nude man touching a naked woman's bare breasts.

Padamsee looked bewildered. The following day, the man returned. 'I am Inspector Kanga,' he introduced himself. Pointing towards *Lovers 1* and *Lovers 2,* he said, 'I am afraid you'll have to remove these two paintings. These images are rather obscene and inappropriate to be shown in a public space.'

Inspector Kanga warned Padamsee of the consequences should he not comply.

'Well, you'll have to present me with a written note,' Padamsee protested. Inspector Kanga dismissed the request for a written notice. He was certain of what had to be done. Four days after his debut solo exhibition in Bombay, on 2 May 1954, Padamsee was arrested by the Vigilance Branch of the Bombay C.I.D.

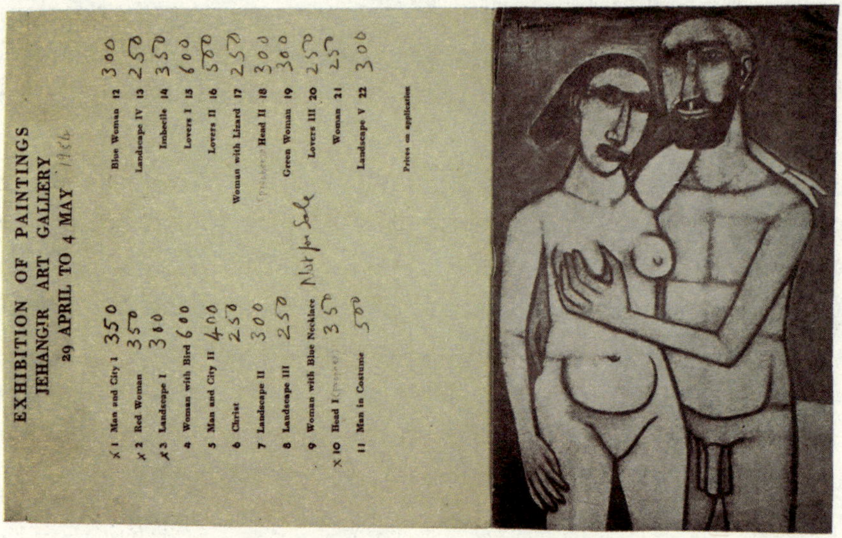

The invite from the Padamsee show depicting Lovers 1 (R)

courtesy of Bhanumati Padamsee Archive, Akbar Padamsee Studio

The officers visited the gallery that morning and confiscated the two paintings Inspector Kanga had declared inappropriate. Convinced that the paintings *Lovers 1* and *Lovers 2* were obscene, Inspector Kanga charged Padamsee under Section 292 of the Indian Penal Code, which prohibits the sale, distribution, or exhibition of obscene materials and carries a penalty of imprisonment or a fine.

Padamsee was furious. And he had every reason to be.

This was not the homecoming reception the 1951 recipient of the *Prix de Noël*—a French government scholarship—had hoped for. In February 1954, Padamsee returned from Paris, having spent three-and-a-half years in the French capital, happily settled in Montparnasse, painting, and holding one-man shows. In Paris, he had discovered his characteristic style. An article in *The Evening News* reported, 'He soon won the recognition of the hoary art-tasters parked on the banks of the Seine, the astute critics who saw and savoured a never-ending cavalcade of European art.'[6]

It was clear very early on that Padamsee was not meant for the family business—the regular occupation and obsession of so many in the Khoja community at that time. That role naturally fell to the older brother by six years, Nooruddin, or Nikki as he was called by friends and family. 'It was my brother who told me, if I believed in the paintings, then as an artist, it is my duty to stand by it,' Padamsee declared.

Padamsee stood by his work. He was charged in the Esplanade Court in Bombay's Fort district. An instinctive expression of love on canvas was deemed obscene by the authorities.

Two days later, Padamsee was granted bail, but the paintings remained in custody of the police.

A defiant Padamsee did not take this incident lying down.

According to Padamsee's lawyer, the artist had decided to 'vindicate his stand' in court and uphold the principle of artistic freedom. In a letter Padamsee wrote after the case was behind him, he stated: 'There is no humiliation in being condemned or sentenced, ostracised, or persecuted... To the extent we do not understand our rights, our rights shall be taken away from us.'

On 4 May 1954, Padamsee even received an encouraging typewritten letter from the firebrand editor Mulk Raj. But this support was passive.

The art scandal became sensational news. 'We tried hard to dissuade Akbar from challenging the Vigilance Branch,' Krishen Khanna recalled. 'But Akbar was a fierce man.'

As tensions mounted during a committee meeting at the Artists' Centre in Bombay's art district, Kala Ghoda, one day, Padamsee angrily declared, 'Those who don't support me can leave; those who do can come with me to jail!'

With that ultimatum Padamsee stormed out. The committee, comprising senior artist Ara, theatre maverick Ebrahim Alkazi and Krishen Khanna grew increasingly concerned. Such zealous rebellion for a 26-year-old artist who had barely cut his teeth in the Indian art world was not viewed as an act of bravado but rather as utter naiveté.

A former art critic with *The Times of India*, R. Chatterji, a conservative man in opinion, was then the secretary at the public space built in 1952 by art patron Cowasji Jehangir Readymoney, where the paintings were exhibited.[7] He was certain that Padamsee was bringing 'disgrace to the art world'. 'But I told them I don't mind losing the case because I was fighting for the rights of the artist,' shared Padamsee, still defiant in his tone.

The conflict between artist and authority, after all, is as old as art itself.

His lawyer, Haribhai Desai, advised finding a strong defence witness. So after Gondhalekar, an adamant Padamsee then approached Emanuel Schlesinger, co-founder of the pharmaceutical company Indo-Pharma Pharmaceuticals Works (INDON), who had sponsored Raza's travels and Husain's work, to defend him in court. Being an ardent patron of Indian art, he seemed like the right contender for the task at hand.

Yet, he turned down Padamsee's request to defend him in court. 'He feared that this would hurt his businesses,' shrugged Padamsee. 'To be honest, I understood his situation. But personally, I felt a bit let down.'

And then came the catalyst that would eventually turn Padamsee's case around.

One morning, Padamsee received an unexpected phone call. It was Rudi on the other side, who by then held a corporate job at Volkart Brothers[8] and was writing regularly for *The Times* publications such as *The Illustrated Weekly of India, The Evening News* and *The Times of India* from 1938 until the 1950s. He had heard about Padamsee's predicament. He conversed fleetingly but sympathetically: 'I hear from the Artists' Centre that you are looking for someone to present a strong point for your case,' he said. 'You don't worry, Padamsee; I'll come to your defence.'

Padamsee, of course, was left speechless.

On 16 June 1954, Rudi took a combative stance in the Court of the Presidency Magistrate, 16th Court, Esplanade, Bombay.

On that fateful day, dressed sharply in a suit, Rudi, a towering figure with a powerful voice and an imposing personality, said in his defence of Padamsee, that the accused was a recognised artist. 'I don't think that it was unusual for an artist of his stature to symbolise human love by the gesture of a male touching a female breast,' he stated.[9] 'This form of symbolising human love could be traced to the art of various countries, including India.'

To substantiate his statement, Rudi, who was also a contributing editor of the art and architecture journal *Marg*, produced photographs of paintings by the Western master Reubens, and the classical sculpture of Italian artist Antonio Canova titled *Psyche Revived by Cupid's Kiss,* where the male hand was touching the female breast.

Rudi drew the court's attention to the cover of the *Archaeological Survey of India* magazine, which showed an image of a sculpture from the Khajuraho temple with a male hand touching a female breast. 'You see, it is an established practice for an artist to symbolise pure and simple human love between man and woman by the gesture of holding the female breast,' said Rudi, as a matter of fact.[10]

Thanks largely to Rudi's testimony, which introduced crucial perspectives on art symbolism, Padamsee won his case.

Excerpts from the copy 'Judgement in the Trial of Akbar Padamsee' declared on 16 June 1954, read:

> 5… In my opinion, painting which is of artistic talent does not become obscene for the simple reason that it contains an expressive pose which in other settings may even be considered objectionable hurt which from the artistic point of view does no more than justice to the subject before the artist… In the pictures before me, the accused has selected as his subject "The Lovers." In doing justice to his subject availed itself certain liberality in respect of expression and pose. As the accused put it in his statement before the Court, in

depicting a subject such as "Lovers", you cannot have a brotherly embrace.

6. Looking at these pictures therefore from the point of the viz. the place where they were exhibited and the people who are normally likely to see such products of artistic talent, the pose, the posture, and the facial expressions which I must say are calm and devoid of any glamour, I fail to see how these pictures can come within the purview of section 292 of the Indian Penal Code. I must therefore acquit the accused. I order accordingly. Bail bond cancelled.

Sd. / M. Nasrullah

An air of triumph filled the staid room as Padamsee expressed his perspective in a handwritten letter after winning the case. He believed that art should not be controlled or directed by policemen but rather entrusted to those who create it and act as custodians of thought and art during their time.

However, the State wasn't convinced with the verdict.

Later that year, an appeal was made by the State of Bombay against the judgement of acquittal passed in favour of the respondent. Padamsee appointed top lawyers of the time—M/s A.A. Peerbhoy, a friend of Husain's—and A.A. Omer, with M/s C.G. Vakil and S.G. Vakil as his advocates.

To determine whether these paintings were obscene, the court found it necessary to examine the context. In this instance, the paintings were displayed at the Jehangir Art Gallery, and the expected audience consisted of individuals interested in art, as opposed to children who were unlikely to visit.

In January 1955, the appeal filed by the State was dismissed. All the exhibits tendered in court by the parties had to be returned to the respective parties. The bond which was executed by the respondent to produce the paintings in the High Court was cancelled.

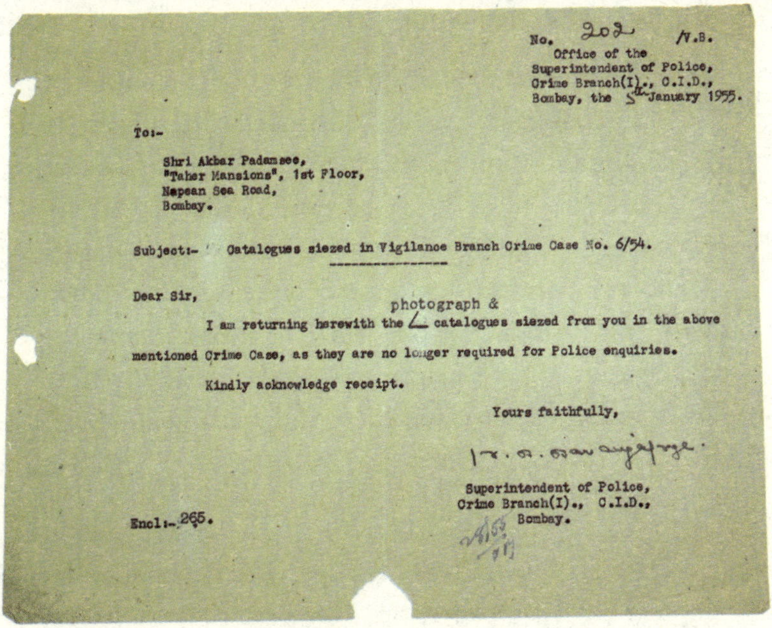

No. 202 /V.B.
Office of the
Superintendent of Police,
Crime Branch(I)., C.I.D.,
Bombay, the 5th January 1955.

To:-

Shri Akbar Padamsee,
"Taher Mansions", 1st Floor,
Napean Sea Road,
Bombay.

Subject:- Catalogues siezed in Vigilance Branch Crime Case No. 6/54.

Dear Sir,

I am returning herewith the photograph & catalogues siezed from you in the above mentioned Crime Case, as they are no longer required for Police enquiries.

Kindly acknowledge receipt.

Yours faithfully,

Superintendent of Police,
Crime Branch(I)., C.I.D.,
Bombay.

Encl:- 265.

The police eventually returned the two paintings to Padamsee

courtesy of Bhanumati Padamsee Archive, Akbar Padamsee Studio

Padamsee's memory served him well, wondering until the present day, 'What about the simple expression of love—a man touching a woman's breasts—was so offensive and threatening to our Indian culture?'[11]

The newly independent nation was grappling with old puritan laws inherited from the British Raj, struggling to define its own cultural identity. Padamsee's refusal to accede to the demands, followed by Rudi's crusade in court, led to a landmark judicial verdict. This, in turn, informed both the police and wielders of art about their respective positions.

Padamsee felt incredibly indebted to Rudi for his staunch defence of the artist's rights. Their mutual friend Krishen Khanna succinctly summarises the episode in the essay, 'To Rudolf von Leyden: A Letter Out of Season', published in *Jewish Exile in India* (*).

In Krishen Khanna's own words:

> No one can forget the formidable defence you put up in the case of obscenity against Padamsee, who had shown an innocuous painting entitled 'Lovers'. You placed the court in a most awkward position by producing photographs of Khajuraho and Konarak. It was put in the most embarrassing position of either sending Akbar to jail and denouncing our 'Ancient Indian Heritage' or accepting Akbar's painting as a valuable addition to that heritage. Akbar won out, so did you and all of us.

✣

When Raza passed away, I was the special art correspondent of a widely-popular city newspaper, the *Mumbai Mirror*, affiliated with *The Times of India*. The newspaper's then-editor, Meenal Baghel, and I thought an interview with the last-surviving PAG member, Krishen Khanna, for the following Sunday's edition would serve as a fitting tribute to his late colleague.

Having had the opportunity to interview Krishen Khanna in the past—when he talked at length of the catastrophic Partition he had witnessed and its memories that translated onto his canvases, or when he spoke about Husain's various peculiarities—I knew that a full-length interview with the nonagenarian, as famous for his art as he is for his most-articulately narrated stories of yore, would surely make for an incisive Sunday read.

I looked forward to hearing his version of the making of the fabled PAG. But the day I reached Krishen Khanna's well-appointed home in Gurgaon, the artist, now 91, was yet to come to terms with Raza's death. 'I feel sad. It is a personal loss to me. One of my dear friends is gone. I have known Raza for a long time and intimately,' he told me. 'But death is inevitable, isn't it? So instead, I look back and think that it is something to rejoice that he has done so much work and left behind a huge legacy, which is not to be trifled with.'

As expected, the veteran artist was generous with his time and tales.

Towards the end of the meeting, as I was waiting for my taxi, he unexpectedly asked me what *The Times* was doing with the writings of his friend, Rudi von Leyden. I looked at him quizzically. I remembered that a couple of hours earlier, during the interview, he had referred to *The Times of India's* former art critic in some context. I couldn't possibly draw a blank. I responded, convinced in my own tone, 'Nothing.'

'You're sitting there; why don't you dip into the archives and pull out his reviews?' he asked.

I nodded sheepishly.

My interview with Krishen Khanna was published on 31 July 2016.

In his account, aside from mentioning Raza, Krishen Khanna spoke about 'Hitler's bounty to India' and how three Second World War émigrés inspired the PAG immensely. Walter Langhammer, a devotee of Oskar Kokoschka, was the art director of *The Times of India* and *The Illustrated Weekly of India*. Rudi, a competent cartoonist gifted with a discerning eye, was the art reviewer for *The Times of India* and *The Evening News*. Then there was Schlesinger, a key patron and companion to many Indian artists. Together, with their trained European eye and knowledge of Western art, they gave the young artists of the time the much-needed impetus and direction in their practice.

However, Rudi, for reasons I found out over multiple interviews with Krishen Khanna later, held a special place in his heart.

✣

Krishen Khanna's suggestion had piqued my curiosity. Taking his advice, I visited the archive room on *The Times* building's second floor between office hours. Stacked with old newspapers, reels of now-defunct publications, meticulously labelled photographs, and books, the room was a researcher's haven. Thankfully, the digitisation of *The Times* had been completed a few years earlier, sparing me the laborious task of going through reels of old—almost faint—paper, as I had done in the case of pulling out articles from its sister publication, *The Evening News*.

I curiously typed 'Rudi von Leyden' into the search.

Only one article popped up—a 1954 court case report that acquitted artist Padamsee on an obscenity charge and described how Rudi stood in his defence.

There would possibly be more articles. Searches for 'R. Leyden', 'R. v. Leyden', 'R.v.L' presented reams and reams of writings.

The plethora of stories left me captivated.

From discovering Raza's talent for drawing in his early days, to reviewing Souza's 'perturbing and bewildering' art show in 1948, to finding the 'intense joy of Ara's paintings', to critiquing PAG's exhibition in Bombay in July 1949, Rudi had written reviews of practically every premier show the group's artists participated in.

Such indispensable historical pieces seemed lost and buried.

Rudi passed away in 1983. Almost four decades later, amidst the manic newsroom moments at the office of *The Times*, known colloquially as the Old Lady of Bori Bunder, I sat researching fervently, in an earnest bid to uncover traces of a legacy that had shaped Indian art history. Later, many art critics who would become names to reckon with—Nissim Ezekiel, Dnyaneshwar Nadkarni, Shanta Gokhale, Roshan Shahani and Ranjit Hoskote—followed in Rudi's footsteps, contributing to the profusion of this history. 'Even though Charles Fabri was there, it was Richard Bartholomew who was the central figure in Delhi. In Bombay, there was no equivalent to Rudi. He wrote pointedly, persuasively and rather well,' said art historian Geeta Kapur.

Surely, there was more to Rudi than his writings.

I contacted Krishen Khanna almost a year later, in May 2017. To my immense luck, he not only remembered me but also the suggestion he had shared about Rudi.

Seizing the moment, I flew to Delhi. It happened to be in the middle of a heatwave. Krishen Khanna's house reflected the weariness of the city's torrid afternoons. The sweltering heat in the room and the stuffy cooler air, typical of a city that can induce slight delirium in the height of summer, only added to the fatigue. However, seated on a brown sofa, Krishen Khanna appeared unusually buoyant. He was not entirely surprised by the serendipity of meeting again to discuss Rudi during peak mango season. 'You know Rudi loved mangoes,' Krishen Khanna smiled, adding, 'And after he left India, he would invariably time his visits during summer to enjoy the fruit.'

Krishen Khanna regaled me with anecdotes and produced a pack of old, circular-shaped, hand-painted Ganjifa cards, once popular in Mughal courts. These intricately designed and richly adorned playing cards, with symbols, motifs and themes reflecting the cultural and artistic diversity of India, were a gift from Rudi. He had a special affinity for these traditional playing cards and would later become one of the leading authorities on Ganjifa. What Krishen Khanna had initially dismissed as a 'stupid hobby' turned to admiration after hearing Rudi's scholarly presentation on the subject. Today, the cherished cards sit with Krishen Khanna in his studio, a fond memento of an old friend.

During that meeting, Krishen Khanna spoke of their familial bond and recounted the episode when Rudi fought tenaciously for the late artist Padamsee over two paintings deemed obscene.

In Krishen Khanna's words, Rudi was not just a critic; he was the 'kingpin of the art world!'

✣

According to art historian and independent curator Yashodhara Dalmia, 'the erudition and meticulousness Rudi brought to his observations was to set the tenor for the years to come.'[12] In a 1982 interview with *The Times*, art critic Dnyaneshwar Nadkarni asked Rudi—who by then had left India—to name younger talents of great promise. Rudi responded that he appreciated the work of Vivan Sundaram[13] as much as he prized that of senior painter Krishen Khanna. 'It was an education to watch Krishen Khanna paint when I met him in Delhi recently,' he said, 'These two Bombay painters, Gieve Patel and Sudhir Patwardhan, are also most impressive, whatever be the exact nature of their ideological belief,' Rudi said. 'And so is Nalini Malani.'[14] The three Bombay artists that Rudi referred to, who were in the nascent stages of their careers, later became artists of much repute. Rudi's intuitive endorsement of their talent when they were barely emerging onto the art scene speaks volumes about his exceptional insight.

Steeped in urban realism, perhaps no one comprehends Bombay through painting quite like Sudhir, a self-taught artist and radiologist. Nalini Malani, shaped by her experiences of migration after the Partition of India and by pressing feminist issues, is today regarded as a pioneer of video art in India. Meanwhile, the late Gieve, a self-taught painter, poet, playwright, polymath and physician, was renowned for his intricate exploration of the human form across the various genres he embraced.

Gieve passed away as I was winding up the final draft of this volume in November 2023. I had met him in 2018 to discuss Rudi's life and work. In 1981, during a visit to Bombay, Rudi phoned the artist, an event he later recounted. Rudi was keen to understand the state of Gieve's practice. At the time, Gieve was working on a painting, *Early Morning Local*, which was later acquired by Chester Herwitz, the American collector, now with the Peabody Essex Museum. When Rudi visited his studio in Colaba, he carefully examined the recent painting and remarked, 'You're quite fond of Piero della Francesca[15], aren't you?' Gieve was indeed impressed by the cool palette of the Italian painter. 'He was judicious enough and could pick up what influences you have,' Gieve recalled.

Rudi knew his artists and his audience well, offering honest, constructive feedback deeply valued by his contemporaries. In one review, Rudi critiqued Krishen Khanna's work; while he recognised his strong sense of colour, he considered his drawing weak. Krishen Khanna took the feedback to heart. 'And for a couple of years, I became more and more monochromatic in my painting, devoting myself entirely to drawing. To the extent that now people think my drawing is much better than my painting,' he said. Rudi's appreciation for Krishen Khanna's drawings evolved gradually, paralleling the slow but steady development of the artist's work. 'He was frank, but he wouldn't kill anyone. He wouldn't demolish anyone's career,' Krishen Khanna said.

Through his observations and writing, Rudi brought perspective to the art movement and refreshingly did not get caught up in jargon or flaunt his prowess as a critic. His feedback, in simple, coherent English, was instrumental in shaping many artistic trajectories.

'His writings weren't academic,' Krishen Khanna pointed out, elaborating: 'A lot of the art writing becomes about the writer who is writing it. It is his/her pouring out, rather than sticking to the objectivity of the work. But Rudi was a man with a conscience. He had a sense of right and wrong.'

✣

This volume is not meant to be a critical appraisal of his writings; rather, it offers an honest retelling of Rudi's life through the prism of art, a life-long passion that not only defined his course but also profoundly impacted the lives he touched.

How does a German, part-Jewish man end up in India ahead of the Second World War and become the 'kingpin' of an art movement?

I spent the following seven years unravelling this *épithète*, retracing an almost-forgotten life and its hidden connections to seismic events through serendipitous encounters across cities and continents. As I delved deeper into Rudi's world, I glimpsed truths much larger than one man's experiences.

CHAPTER ONE

The Catalyst

It was a regular working day at the spacious office on the third floor of *The Times of India* building in 2003, with scribes peering into their screens and furiously typing out the day's breaking news. The routine hustle was suddenly disrupted by the arrival of a perplexing brown paper envelope addressed to 'Mr. Rudi von Leyden'. The package was so intriguing that the correspondents mentioned it in *The Times of India*'s 'Citylights' column the following week.

> *The Times* correspondents are quite used to letters and press releases that continue to arrive for editors who have long left or retired from the building. Shanta Gokhale, Arts Editor, still gets mail, as do Fatima Zakaria and Khushwant Singh. But last week, a plump brown envelope drew gasps of disbelief. It was neatly addressed to 'Rudi Von Leyden, The Art Critic, The Times of India'.
>
> Those who recognise the name will react with similar incredulity. For Rudolf von Leyden, a Jewish refugee in Bombay, was the art critic of this newspaper, not in the near past, but in the decades before and after the Second World War. In the thirty-odd years that he lived in Bombay (1930s to the 1960s), he played

a seminal role in nurturing India's nascent modernist art movement, frontlined by Souza, Husain, Raza, Ara and the other grandees of the Progressive Artists' Group. He was a tall, elegant German, so up-to-speed with the cultural currents in Europe, who critiqued the brush strokes of Husain and Raza.

One of Leyden's close friends was Kekoo Gandhy of Gallery Chemould, himself a mentor to many struggling artists in post-war Bombay. Gandhy remembers how Rudi used to attend an art opening at the town hall and "rush to the Times office on his bicycle to file his review so that it appeared in the next morning's paper." Berlin's loss, says Gandhy, was Bombay's gain. To return to the square envelope. It was from a Mrs. Mili Mukherjee, daughter of the late artist D. K. Roy Chowdhury (1926 to 2005). The CD contained an invitation to an exhibition of his works in Delhi. Chowdhury, a scholarly painter travelled widely through Europe, was fascinated with murals, Mondrian and Rembrandt, and embraced modernism over the genteel style of the Bengal school.

Regrettably, Herr R von Leyden was unable to cycle over with his notebook and unsparing eye.[16]

✣

Rudi's story begins nearly seven decades prior. The year was 1933. The writing was on the wall. Germany was about to transition from democracy to dictatorship.

Heinrich Himmler, one of most powerful men in Nazi Germany and known as the chief architect of the Holocaust, was appointed

Rudi in his 20s in Germany

police president. This ushered in a wave of violence as nearly 5,000 opponents of Nazism were arrested in Bavaria. By May, over 2,033 had been taken to the newly constructed Dachau concentration camp. Meanwhile, the German general and statesman who led the Imperial German Army during World War I, President Paul von Hindenburg, had only recently appointed Hitler as Chancellor.[17]

What followed was a series of calamitous events including the Reichstag fire. Soon after, Hitler assumed absolute power with a clear plan to eliminate political opposition and establish Germany as a unified one-party state. This transformation, however, came at a tremendous cost to human life.

Numerous minority groups, such as Jehovah's Witnesses, Roma people, homosexuals and individuals with disabilities, were imprisoned or killed during the Holocaust. But a majority of the victims were those with communist leanings and of Jewish heritage.

Rudi, then a 24-year-old PhD student of Geology at the University of Göttingen, fitted both criteria.

Rudi's youngest brother, Wolfgang von Leyden, gave an account of these events in his memoir, *Growing Up Under the Weimar Republic,*

1918-1933: Reflections on Personal Identity and the Past. Wolfgang admitted that while he was not swayed by Communist ideology, his brother Rudi had joined the *Deutsche Kommunistische Partei* (German Communist Party) ranks, actively engaging in their discussions and demonstrations. 'If he had not been my brother, I would have regarded his enthusiasm and activities with dismay. Yet, I did nothing to dissuade him from his political beliefs,' Wolfgang wrote.

Like Rudi, Wolfgang, who later taught philosophy at the University of Durham for over thirty years, also studied in Göttingen. However brief his time there—lasting just two semesters—it presented a blend of a charming town, an idyllic countryside, parochial residents, and a host of internationally renowned academics.

One evening, as Wolfgang dined in a *Rathskeller* (the term in German-speaking countries for a bar or restaurant situated in the basement of a city hall or nearby), a young man clad in the black uniform of the Nazi storm troopers approached him, offered a 'Heil Hitler' salute, and exclaimed abruptly, 'You're the von Leyden! I need to discuss matters with you.'

Wolfgang, interpreting this as a dire and awkward situation, presumed the man was mistaking him for his brother, Rudi, known for his political activism. Unsure how to proceed, he cautiously initiated a conversation.

The man, a prominent figure in the Nazi hierarchy, delivered a shock: 'Plans are being made to shoot you, or at least to beat you up, if you show yourself again in political demonstrations as one of the ringleaders of the Göttingen Communist Party.'

Wolfgang clarified with some trepidation that he was not 'the' von Leyden, but rather, it was his brother who held that distinction.

The Nazi, now slightly fazed by the revelation, quickly changed his tone from contemptuous to courteous. 'Well, then please pass on my information to your brother and let him know that I respect him and would like to have a good talk with him about politics,' he said.

When Rudi returned to Göttingen, Wolfgang told him about the encounter. Rudi, who had already heard about the new man in the opposite camp, promised to look him up. Upon meeting the Nazi, he found him to be an 'intelligent and decent man'. Rudi was indebted to him for the information that might spare his skin, if not his life. He promised to be more careful when appearing in public as a party member.

Although the brothers were close, Rudi rarely talked about his personal matters. However, during a brief stay at Wolfgang's place in Göttingen, he suddenly announced his plans to visit Berlin: 'I have met this girl in Berlin, who possesses the three most attractive features as far as I am concerned—she is pretty, she is a Communist, and she is a sculptress.'

Eager to see the woman with whom he was in love, Rudi departed for the weekend but returned prematurely, visibly tormented. Wolfgang, by his own admission, had never seen his brother in such anguish.[18] As it turned out, when Rudi arrived at his girlfriend's flat in Berlin, he found her with his best friend, who was also a Communist. Rudi had introduced them during his last visit.

After his girlfriend confessed to falling in love with another man, he felt shattered. This heartbreak came at a time when Rudi already felt despair about the political climate in Germany. Despite his pain, it seemed like his family's esteemed position might shield him from the rising tide of Nazism.

The von Leydens were a highly respected family. Rudi's paternal grandfather, Professor Ernst von Leyden, was a renowned Berlin physician knighted by Kaiser Frederick III and memorialised with a statue, re-erected at the Charité campus in 2019. His grandmother founded the German Women's Club, and Rudi's father, Victor, followed a typical professional path for his class, becoming a Doctor of Law, an officer in WWI, and rising within the government.

Rudi's mother, Luise von Leyden, was a baptised Christian and a former Red Cross nurse with Jewish roots in the notable Reichenheim family. Born in 1883 to Julius Reichenheim and Anna Eisner, she was classified as a 'full Jew' under the Nuremberg Laws.[19] The Reichenheims traced their lineage to the Brandenburg District near Magdeburg, having embraced Christianity when their first child was born. However, Luise's Jewish ancestry would make her a 'full Jew' under the Nuremberg Laws, exposing Rudi to danger as a 'half-Jew' in 1933.

One day, Rudi's worst fears manifested themselves. Several of Rudi's friends, aware of the imminent crisis in Germany, hurried to him exclaiming, 'You must disappear. The Gestapo (the ever-vigilant, brutal secret police of Nazi Germany and German-occupied Europe) is after you!'[20]

Rudi immediately sought the counsel of his family. Together, they decided that it would be safer for him to relocate to Bombay, India, where his older brother Albrecht resided. Albrecht had been living in India since 1927, overseeing the photographic section at the Dutch company that acted for I.G. Farben, the German conglomerate of eight leading chemical manufacturers, including Bayer, Hoechst, and BASF—the largest of their kind at the time. Albrecht, who was well-established in Bombay, recommended that Rudi stay with him for a few months until conditions back home improved. Meanwhile, Wolfgang left for Florence, hopeful of completing his studies there.

On 22 May 1933, Rudi boarded the cargo ship *S.S. Ockenfels* in Antwerp, bound via Port Said for Bombay Harbour.

Life on the ship, as recounted in Rudi's descriptive letters to his mother—whom he addressed as 'Mamsi'—wasn't particularly pleasant. He worked in the mornings under a rather 'bossy' captain who was not the most genial person aboard. The first engineer, who was the only nice person aboard, sang arias from Lohengrin or Parsifal with a roaring voice across the ocean in the evenings. He also worked on a paper on geology and completed it upon reaching Bombay.

Shortly before his arrival in Bombay, Rudi dashed off another letter to his Mamsi, sharing his considerable curiosity about India, where the parents had journeyed in 1909.

Rudi with Albrecht in 1933

Bombay was a stark contrast to the growing turmoil in Germany. The rise of Nazism and the onset of its anti-Semitic pogrom appeared to have had little impact on British-occupied India—not even among the German community in Bombay, governed by Consul Kapp. Unlike many European Jewish refugees who sought asylum or stopped en route to Shanghai, Rudi's arrival on the Indian shores wasn't dictated by strange fate; it was the result of a well-thought-out, convenient plan. Though heartbroken for more than one reason, he entered the city by the sea comfortably.

A swarm of warm air and the intoxicating smell of the sea greeted Rudi's arrival at the Bombay Harbour in June 1933.

Nestled along the western shores of India, Bombay in the 1930s was a captivating blend of cultures, where British colonial influence mingled with indigenous traditions to create a tapestry of life that exuded vibrancy from every corner. The British-occupied port city was, quite literally, the gateway to India.

A Christmas greeting card illustrated by Rudi sums up his time in India in 1933

Rudi's first days were unsettling, yet exciting.

An avid mountaineer, Albrecht was keen for Rudi to experience India in all its splendour and planned multiple travels for him, including a memorable trip to Kashmir. Rudi was impressed by the scenic beauty of Kashmir, particularly during his hike to Mt. Haramukh in the Ganderbal district of Jammu and Kashmir. From there, he witnessed the fabulous view of Nanga Parbat. Rudi shared his immense knowledge of Northwest India's tectonics with his Mamsi through drawings in his letters. These illustrations, a regular feature in his correspondence with her, were intended to bring a smile to her face during these uncertain times.

The brothers travelled to Delhi and Agra and soaked in the sights and sounds of the country, which Rudi beautifully summed up in his annual Christmas greeting card to his family back in Germany, where the situation was becoming increasingly grim.

A painting by Albrecht von Leyden of his Pali Hill Home

Rudi lived with Albrecht in a bungalow at 17 Pali Hill, with expansive views of the Arabian Sea. Albrecht worked in the bustling Fort district of Bombay and had selected Pali Hill for its cooler climate and tranquillity compared to the city centre. Dara Gandhy, a long-time Bombay resident, remembered Pali Hill as tree-lined with numerous bungalows, tennis courts and a golf club.

Though golf seemed to be the preferred sport in the neighbourhood, the brothers—especially Albrecht—took a fancy to horse-riding. They spent their time socialising with fellow expatriates, dining out and swimming in the pristine waters of Juhu Beach to get respite from the heat. To occupy himself, Rudi helped Albrecht with an article on the Haramukh expedition, complete with photos, for *The Times of India.*

Although Rudi knew that the situation back home was bleak and the possibility of finding a suitable job in geology was practically nil, he remained optimistic about his future. He applied for work as a geologist in South Africa but didn't get a response for a long time. A life in India seemed like a pragmatic choice. And though

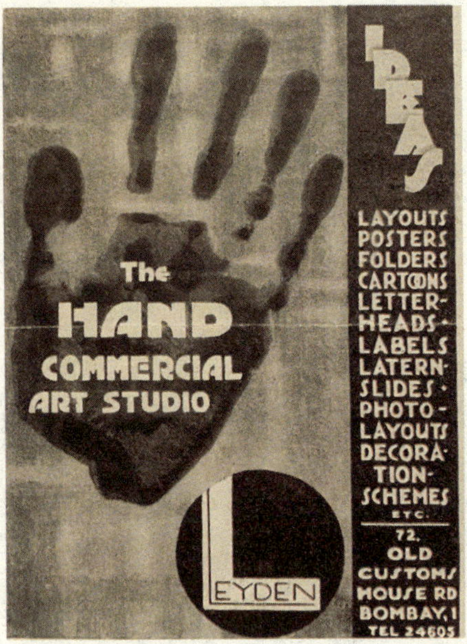

The Advt. for Rudi's studio

Albrecht had a corporate job, Rudi did not want to depend on his elder brother's benevolence.

As an amateur artist, Rudi began using his skills to design advertisements, posters, invitation cards and menus for friends. Encouraged by these initial successes and some monetary help from the new friends he made, Rudi set up an advertising studio called the 'The Hand Commercial Art Studio' almost a year into his arrival in Bombay.

Rudi set up his workplace on the ground floor of an old building on Old Customs House Road. In a 1979 essay, he spoke about his initial days in India, remarking that his workplace wasn't the most pleasant environment. The stench from a municipal refusal dump and the dust of the tobacco warehouses located nearby filled the room. Besides, the rattling printing press at the back of the building ensured that the place was never quiet. Rudi found a comrade in Faustin Baptista, a young commercial artist who struggled alongside him. Together, they learned a great deal about their trade.

Choose art or geology?

In a letter addressed to his mother in July 1935, Rudi expressed his desire to pursue art full-time but felt torn since he had spent more than a decade training in geology and found himself at a crossroads.

Somewhere, he hoped that all these torments would eventually lead to a meaningful profession.[21] But his failed attempts at finding a job in geology left him deeply disappointed. To illustrate this conundrum, he drew a man looking at two signboards—one directing him to geology, and the other to art.

One day, at a charity event, Rudi found himself at the same table as the manager in the advertising department of *The Times of India* publications, Frank Coulton. He was accompanied by his wife and a few of his friends. A person at the table was impressed by the well-designed programme card. When asked, Rudi shyly admitted that he was the designer.

A few weeks later, Rudi received a phone call from Frank Coulton. 'I want to offer you a "badlee" (a temporary position in lieu of someone else) job at *The Times of India's* layout department for six months, while one of our English employees is on home leave,' he said.

✣

With Hitler in power, the prospect of returning to Germany was uncertain. Rudi accepted Frank Coulton's offer to work temporarily in the advertisement department of *The Times of India*. He quickly sent another letter—dated 6 April 1936—to his mother, informing her about the job, which he saw as an opportunity to hone his skills.

At *The Times*, Rudi joined a large, competent team. Nearly twenty artists crowded within the cramped workspace. Rudi was working with a pool of talent, excelling in figure work, lettering, and in making swift show roughs for the 'reps' to take to clients. Some of these artists became luminaries in the advertising world in the years to come. V.N. Adarkar, for instance, became head of the Commercial Art Section of the Sir J.J.School of Art and later Dean of its sister institution, Sir J.J.School of Applied Art. Victor Fernandez and the Salgaonkar brothers became leading art directors; Jekule later ran his own prosperous printing press, while Ratan Batra's eponymous advertising firm was one of the best known.

In a later essay written by Rudi, he reminisced about his old team at the newspaper: 'Mr. Tom Bagnall was head of the layout department, Harold Taylor was head of art, and Alex Tailor, a rather friendly chap, sat in the corner doing illustrations, cartoons and drawing images of Santa Claus for full page advertisements of the Great Western Stores and other providers of goodies during Christmas season.'

The routine for Rudi, the junior boy, who by now was in his late twenties, was to make 'pencil roughs' for the typesetting department. This division was ruled by Mr. Turner, a mighty and greatly feared Englishman who, as legend has it, never moved from behind his desk in a cabin in the middle of the typesetting shop.

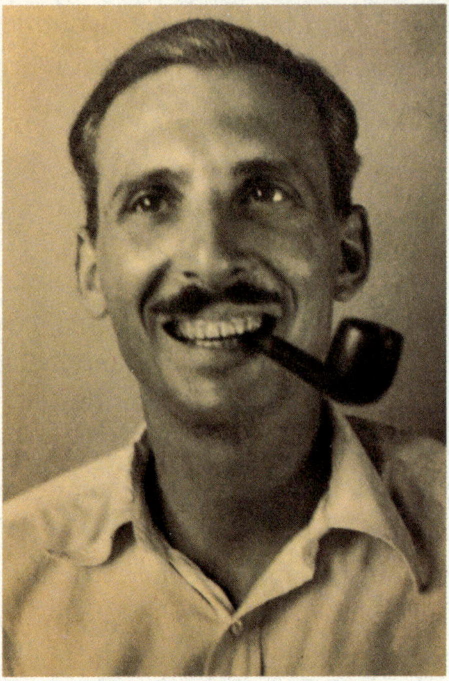

Rudi in Bombay in the 1940s

The efficiency of that department was astonishing. The advertising canvassers, or 'reps', would appear first thing in the morning and their requests were placed on Rudi's table, one after another. He was managing twenty to thirty advertising requests each morning, consisting of brief notes from clients specifying their requirements, and the date of publishing, which was invariably the next day.

Rudi's job at *The Times of India* wasn't clearly defined, and his tasks ranged from brainstorming headlines, selling arguments, and devising a reasonable layout in a space normally far too small for the message to be accommodated, to marking the type to be used and getting two lines of copy from the copywriter—a gentleman by the name of Mr. Carpenter. The layout would go to Turner's boys, who would have 'hand proofs' ready when the reps set out on their afternoon rounds. Advertising, in those days, meant labouring over copies for long hours.

Since it was a temporary substitute position, Rudi only spent his precious morning hours at *The Times*. The paper couldn't employ more Europeans as a mandate. Although this disappointed Albrecht, Rudi hoped to secure a permanent job at *The Times*. Meanwhile, he continued running his own small-scale design studio while integrating into Bombay's cultural circles.

With Albrecht holding a high-ranking corporate job, Rudi had access to an affluent group, who were interested in pushing the aesthetic dialogue in the city forward. In these circles, Rudi's natural flair for the arts was encouraged, and his opinion on art was held in high esteem—well before he formally started writing as a critic in 1938.

In May 1936, the European Progressive Group invited Rudi to speak at a meeting on the subject of 'East and West in the World History of Art'.

Rudi believed it had taken longer to recognise Indian, Chinese, or Persian art as art compared to Medieval European, Romanesque and Gothic art, which was rediscovered in the last century.

> All of this was classified as primitive, exotic or barbarous and had its place in history or ethnography, but not in the history of art. Modern art history has changed this outlook and the arts and crafts of far remote civilisations are known to us today as being equal or more beautiful and more refined than those of Greece or Rome... Our knowledge of prehistoric civilisations and those wide movements of people from East to West and West to East throughout the ages attempts to find a common platform or platforms, different styles and types of art and to envisage them in the comprehensive framework of the world history of art. Today we stand at the beginning of this new method and too much still is mere theory, but a few big outlines seem to appear and mark themselves as all-important.[22]

The lecture was decidedly informative; the only complaint was that it wasn't supported by a presentation with pictorial references.

⁘

Far away in Germany, Hitler became more and more unassailable. It was the letters that the Leydens exchanged that vividly capture this significant shift. They wrote to one another regularly—it gave them the notion of safety and security, perhaps. Today, it's these tangible documents that not only serve as a repository of their personal histories, but also provide an insight into the social constructs of the time.

In a letter dated 14 December 1936, now preserved by his niece Flora Veit-Wild, a researcher based in Berlin, Rudi communicated the sorrow of spending a fourth Christmas away from home. But he also expressed that despite all the odds, he felt strangely close to his family, having gone through everything together, yet building their own lives.

As Rudi had foretold, and as we learnt through a later correspondence with his mother, he secured a permanent job with *The Times of India* in February 1937. He signed a three-year contract as a full-time assistant.

But just before immersing himself full-time in *The Times* office, he took up a special assignment with the British tour company, Thomas Cook. Rudi served as an escort for a group of tourists from Colombo, Sri Lanka, guiding them through India for about four weeks. He detailed these adventures in an eight-page letter to his mother, describing the places they visited, the challenges they faced, the conflicts within the group and the fantastic landscapes they witnessed.

Back from his trip, Rudi became a regular at *The Times*' layout department. Around the same time, two remarkable additions were made in the department—Ernest Banbury, an artist and cartoonist of merit, and Bill Williams, the new copywriter and a fantastic friend who taught Rudi more about English poetry and literature than anybody else. Together with fellow expatriate Rufus Gibson and the brilliant Frank Moraes, who'd go on to become the first Indian editor of *The Times of India*, and others, Rudi formed a gang that lived it up in Bombay.

The group held animated discussions through long nights, attended the cinema, and feasted on scrumptious fare, including Moghlai Murgi at Georges on Apollo Street and at The Star of Asia, another popular joint on the busy Sandhurst Road. They also viewed art shows at The Taj Mahal Palace Hotel, in downtown Bombay.

On one such evening in June, Rudi stumbled upon an exhibition at the Taj that would eventually change not only the course of his own life but also the trajectory of Indian modern art.

It wasn't the most inspiring show Rudi had seen, yet he felt moved enough to share his views with his colleagues.

He spoke so passionately that Simon Pereira, the editor of *The Evening News*, who had previously noticed Rudi's talent for drawing and published his cartoons regularly in the paper, felt compelled to ask, 'Why don't you review the show for the paper?'

Rudi von Leyden, the art critic, was born.

On 11 June 1938, *The Evening News* published a review by 'RVL', titled 'Indian Art on View at the Taj Mahal Hotel'. The works on display were a collection of pictures, drawings, and paintings by two brothers, Sarada and Ranada Ukil, who were students at the Art School in Delhi, now considered sought-after artists.

The show looked promising, and Rudi candidly shared his views.

Since then, Rudi routinely wrote art reviews for *The Evening News*, later in *The Times of India* and *The Illustrated Weekly of India*. He attended every art show in the city in an official capacity and filed his copies the same day. Kekoo Gandhy, a frequent visitor at art openings, would regularly find Rudi scampering back after spending enough time viewing the art display. ‘I asked him once why he did this and he said that the artist had worked so hard, put in years of time and the least he could do was make sure that they woke up the next day to find his review in the paper.’[23]

Rudi indeed became an authority on Indian art.

Who could have possibly foretold that ‘the’ von Leyden whom the Nazis were after in Germany would become ‘the’ word on art in India?

CHAPTER TWO

Bombay, A Home in Exile

The excitement in the air was palpable.

A record crowd of 4,000 gathered at the Cooperage (Football) Ground, one of the largest stadiums in Bombay, to cheer on the Gymkhana Ladies XI. The gallant team, representing the Bombay Gymkhana, defeated the 'Rest of Bombay XI' in the city's first official women's hockey match. The charity match, played in aid of Their Majesties' Silver Jubilee Fund, collected a generous sum of Rs. 8,000 in March 1935.

> It was a great game, played at a fast pace throughout, and one in which some really good hockey was witnessed. Neither of the three hockey "stars" let down the public. Jenny played a wonderful game displaying amazing stickwork and activity, while Miss von Leyden ran her very close in being the outstanding player on the field.[24]

This Miss von Leyden was none other than Rudi's younger sister, Victoria, a hockey player of great merit. She received glowing reviews from the press. 'Great Game by Miss Sandison and Miss von Leyden,' read the first line of *The Times of India* report published on 8 March 1935.

Rudi, one of the witnesses to her momentous match, illustrated the enthralling event for *The Evening News*.

Image of the cartoon published in The Evening News *on 8 March 1935*

courtesy of Rudi's scrapbook; Gulam Mohammed Sheikh; Asia Art Archive

Victoria had previously played women's hockey in Berlin but was barred from the German national team because of her Jewish heritage. Bombay was her great escape. Besides, Victoria's parents didn't wish for her to be with her much-older boyfriend Otto, who lived in the same German city.

She was all of twenty-one when her parents sent her off to stay with Rudi and Albrecht in Bombay, in the hope that she might forget Otto. After Otto gave her an ultimatum to return, the two eventually got married on 9 July 1935, in Garmisch-Partenkirchen, a splendid Alpine town in Bavaria.

Her daughter Flora revealed: 'My mother always told me that her parents found my father too old for her and that he had a bad reputation because he was previously divorced and was untrustworthy in matters related to women.'

The Leyden siblings would go horse riding in Bombay in 1935

Rudi's and Albrecht's letters to their mother were explicit—they tried to dissuade their sister from seeing Otto, hoping she would let go of him and instead marry a German man named Buschow, whom she was dating during her time in Bombay. He also played hockey, and the brothers thought he was more suited for her.

Buschow was the opposite of Otto, who was demanding, complicated, and had too much power over the young woman. In their letters to their mother, the brothers criticised their sister's behaviour and her lack of effort to introduce Otto to her parents so that their relationship could receive their blessing. 'Even while she was in India, he avoided meeting the Leyden parents, so they say,' Flora said. Victoria's parents encouraged her to socialise with other men and participate in various sports activities during her time in India. Victoria enjoyed her time thoroughly—the sports, the society, the works.

A story she often shared with her children was about one of her boyfriends, who promised her a gold bangle for each goal she would score in the matches. Once, she scored eighteen. For a long time, she wore five of the bangles, and then passed them on to Flora. The other thirteen were used directly for gold teeth fillings during the war years.

In addition to playing hockey, Victoria was passionate about horse riding. Considering her stature, Albrecht even purchased a smaller horse for her, allowing all three siblings to ride together on numerous hunting trips.

Victoria's passion for sports did enrich her time in India, and she was instrumental in introducing women's hockey in colonial Bombay.

That sports illustration by Rudi, which featured Victoria, was spotted by *The Illustrated Weekly of India's* sprightly editor, Stanley Jepsen. Impressed with his skill, Stanley offered to publish a series of Rudi's cartoons on Bombay clubs. Later, Stanley also encouraged Rudi to create cartoons on the political climate in the world for his news magazine.

From 1938 until 1947, Rudi's cartoons were prominently featured in a four-column space in the weekly. He made Hitler, the German demagogue, the target of most of his cartoons during the war years and the time preceding them.

A well-known radiologist in Mumbai, Dr. Hemant Morparia, who has contributed his perceptive cartoons across several publications for over two decades, observed that Rudi's ink-and-brush illustrations appeared deeply influenced by David Low, a legendary political cartoonist and caricaturist.

The New Zealand-born, UK-bred illustrator was renowned for his satirical work in London's *Evening Standard*. His notable depictions included the controversial Italian dictator and founder of fascism, Benito Mussolini; Joseph Stalin, the dictator of the Union of Soviet Socialist Republics (USSR); and Hitler. Additionally, his work critiqued British Prime Minister Neville Chamberlain's policy of appeasement towards Hitler.

Rudi primarily focused his satirical illustrations on critiquing the situation in Germany during that period. In *The Illustrated Weekly of India's* 1944 cartoon 'It looks like a White Christmas',

Rudi was the political cartoonist with
The Illustrated Weekly of India *from 1938 to 1947*

a rather perturbed Hitler is depicted staring at a white strand of hair marked as Denmark, signifying Germany's weakening grip on the country, which was experiencing significant civil unrest, further compounding his troubles. Rudi's cartoons weren't apparently farcical but seemed more like propaganda against the Nazi regime.[25]

On the other hand, his cartoons on India reflected his empathy towards its natives, without offending the British. He drew what he saw, and despite being a white 'sahib', he didn't exoticise or satirise the locals, nor did he patronise them.

He created these cartoons under the moniker 'Denley', an anagram of his surname, to ensure that his family back home didn't face the wrath of the Nazis due to his illustrations.

Rudi's unforgettable time at *The Times* was marked not only by professional highs but also the enduring personal camaraderie he enjoyed both inside and outside of the newsroom.
Austrian artist Walter Langhammer was one such lifelong friend.

A sketch of Rudi and Langhammer by the latter

Born in 1905 in Graz, Austria, Langhammer fled to Bombay after the National Socialist annexation of Austria in 1938. Langhammer's wife, Käthe Urbach, was Jewish, and Austria was no longer safe for them. The couple left Austria after the death of his father-in-law, Otto Urbach, a German-Jewish social democrat.

Langhammer, who had studied under Ferdinand Andri, Hans Tichy and Josef Jungwirth at the Vienna Academy of Fine Arts, was already a well-established artist in Vienna.[26]

In addition to his anti-Nazi stance, Langhammer's political beliefs manifested through his satirical caricatures. Their journey to the subcontinent was catalysed by the persistence of a spirited Parsi girl named Silloo Vakil.[27] In Yashodhara Dalmia's exhaustive volume, she is referred to as Shirin Vimadalal.[28]

Silloo, an ardent admirer of Langhammer's work, urged him to visit India with unwavering determination. With Hitler's shadow cast over Austria, Langhammer sought refuge in the subcontinent. He penned a letter to Silloo, explaining his situation. Silloo, who came from an influential family, convinced *The Times* editor Francis Low to grant Langhammer a job.

Langhammer, accompanied by his wife Käthe, set foot on Indian soil, and found himself appointed as the inaugural art director of *The Times of India*. He introduced the publication's annual colour edition, capturing the vivid hues of India in a tapestry of visual storytelling. Langhammer was an artist in love with the kaleidoscope of colours and the boundless light that enveloped the subcontinent.

In Rudi, he found a fellow art believer with a common history.

That the two would mentor a group of artists who would become the most sought-after names in the Indian art scene speaks to a story of destiny's divine timing. Indeed, their dynamic and collective impact on the artistic oeuvres of some of the most venerable names in the art world is a recurring theme in the subsequent chapters. Kekoo Gandhy was one such stalwart who owed his early understanding of modern art to the two.

> I can't say honestly that I was interested in art to begin with, or that I had any great knowledge of it. I got interested through my friends Langhammer and Leyden, after seeing their great enthusiasm for contemporary Indian art. I was moved by their belief in the future of Indian contemporary art. And once I began interacting with the artists—they were such beautiful, trusting people, Ara and Raza and Hebbar—I felt I could be a go-between.[29]

Kekoo Gandhy's efforts, along with those of his wife Khorshed, in championing the arts led to the establishment of Gallery Chemould one of India's premier contemporary art institutions. This story is delightfully captured by writer Jerry Pinto in his book *Citizen Gallery*.

These overlapping narratives serve as a poignant reminder of our shared human connections.

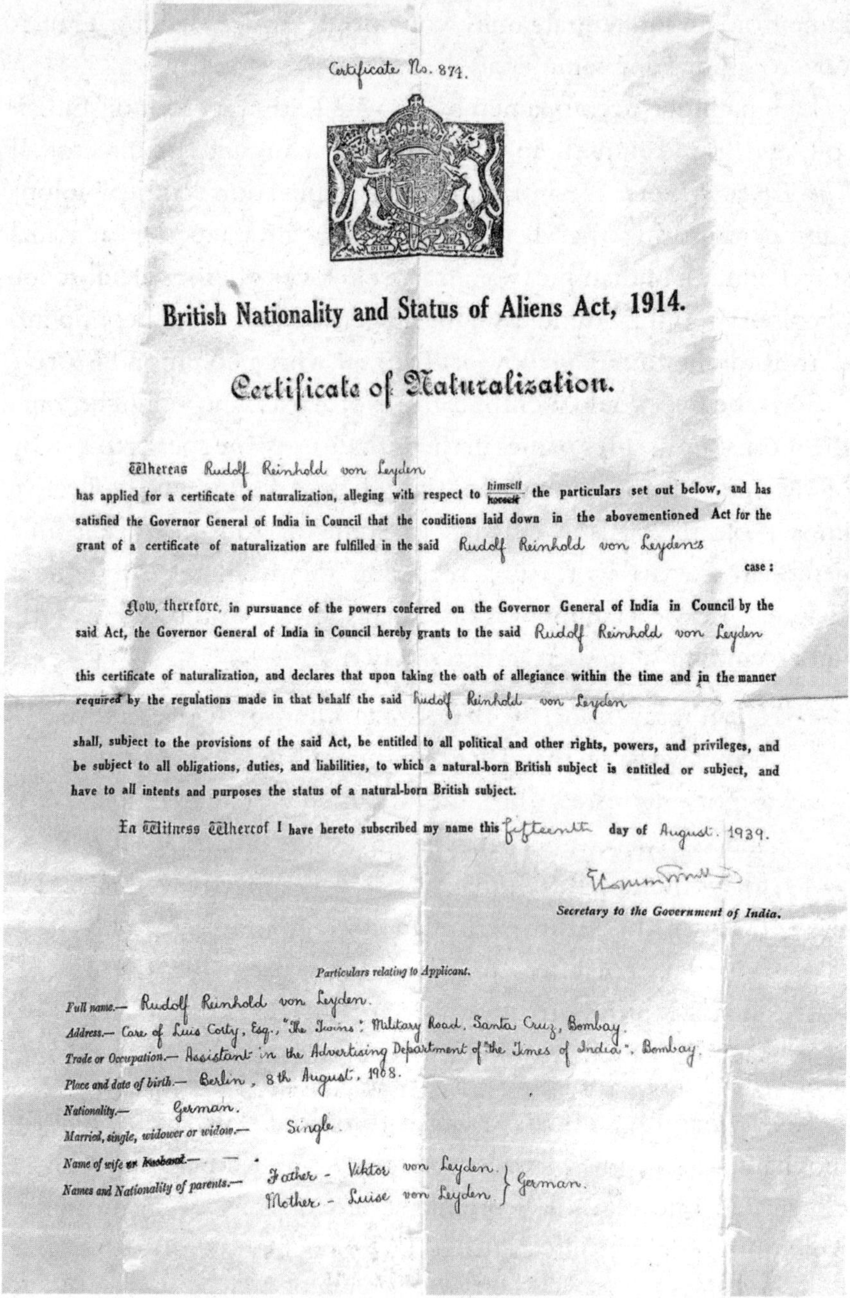

Certificate No. 874.

British Nationality and Status of Aliens Act, 1914.

Certificate of Naturalization.

Whereas Rudolf Reinhold von Leyden has applied for a certificate of naturalization, alleging with respect to himself ~~herself~~ the particulars set out below, and has satisfied the Governor General of India in Council that the conditions laid down in the abovementioned Act for the grant of a certificate of naturalization are fulfilled in the said Rudolf Reinhold von Leyden's case:

Now, therefore, in pursuance of the powers conferred on the Governor General of India in Council by the said Act, the Governor General of India in Council hereby grants to the said Rudolf Reinhold von Leyden this certificate of naturalization, and declares that upon taking the oath of allegiance within the time and in the manner required by the regulations made in that behalf the said Rudolf Reinhold von Leyden shall, subject to the provisions of the said Act, be entitled to all political and other rights, powers, and privileges, and be subject to all obligations, duties, and liabilities, to which a natural-born British subject is entitled or subject, and have to all intents and purposes the status of a natural-born British subject.

In Witness Whereof I have hereto subscribed my name this fifteenth day of August. 1939.

Secretary to the Government of India.

Particulars relating to Applicant.

Full name.— Rudolf Reinhold von Leyden.
Address.— Care of Luis Corty, Esq., "The Twins", Military Road, Santa Cruz, Bombay.
Trade or Occupation.— Assistant in the Advertising Department of "The Times of India", Bombay.
Place and date of birth.— Berlin, 8th August, 1908.
Nationality.— German.
Married, single, widower or widow.— Single.
Name of wife ~~or husband~~.— —
Names and Nationality of parents.— Father - Viktor von Leyden, Mother - Luise von Leyden } German.

Rudi's certificate of naturalisation in 1939

War was looming over Europe. Both Albrecht and Rudi, who by then had sought British citizenship, agreed that their parents should relocate to Bombay until the situation normalised.

Albrecht, like Rudi, had considered the possibility of acquiring British nationality by naturalisation. In one of his diary notes from 1979, Albrecht wrote: 'After thirty years of a loyal and successful career as a civil servant and four-and-a-half years of service in World War I on the Western front during which he was wounded three times and decorated with the Iron Cross, my father was dismissed in 1933. I felt strongly that I had adequate reasons to cast off my German nationality.' The only bond remaining for him was a feeling of loyalty towards his employers, who had given him no reason to doubt their commitment to an old employee. However, the annexation of Austria by Hitler in March 1938 erased any uncertainty about the way forward. 'This convinced me that Hitler meant war, as only a look at the map of Europe, made it clear that free Czechoslovakia, now encircled by Nazi armies from three sides, could not last much longer and that this would result in a World War,' Albrecht reasoned.

To be naturalised in India, one had to have resided in the country for at least five years, the last twelve months of which had to be continuous. The application for naturalisation had to be sponsored by two British-born subjects before the Chief Presidency Magistrate. A day or two after Hitler's takeover of Austria, Rudi and Albrecht received an invitation from their close friends, Wilfrid Russell and John Gough, to dinner at the elite Willingdon Sports Club—a recreational space largely favoured by the British and the Indian Maharajas at that time. Both Wilfrid and John were prominent figures within Bombay's business and social circles, having attended prestigious institutions in Oxford, and Cambridge. The dinner was a pleasant one, with a specially printed menu of excellent food and wine. 'Quite suddenly, aware that I was to face the crossroads of fate, my mind was made up. I asked my two English friends if they would sponsor my application for naturalisation. They agreed most readily, and the evening ended with toasts to our mutual future.'

Within a few days, Albrecht's contact, an Anglo-Indian police officer, Colin Neale, had prepared the necessary papers, and Wilfrid, John and he went to the Court. The formalities were quickly completed, and the application was sent on its way to Delhi and Shimla. Rudi was naturalised in August 1939.

Retrospectively, Albrecht believed that he had taken the right decision. He remarked in his notes:

> Not to apply at this juncture would have led me in September 1939 into internment as an enemy alien as by then the Second World War was in full progress. I would have been unable to start a new career in business until after the war and I would have been in no position to support my parents when the Nazis drove them into exile in November 1938.

The Nazis had persecuted Luise for her Jewish ancestry and forcibly retired her husband from his roles as Ministerial Director in the Prussian Ministry of Interior and as President of the Administrative Court. In 1935, they moved from Berlin to the house they had built in Garmisch-Partenkirchen. The Leyden house, situated at Hölzleweg 11 in the old village of Partenkirchen, was a favourite gathering place for the family. Here, they spent quality time together, surrounded by the dominant and scenic panorama of the mountains. Flora fondly remembered the short trek from the Leyden home up to the hill, where St. Anton's Chapel is still located. 'Inside the chapel, there was a little machine with a slot for coins. If you put a coin in, little Jesus will come to the front and greet you. This had always been such a pleasure for us kids and even later,' Flora recalled.

Of the five children, the second oldest, Albrecht (born 1905) had already emigrated to Bombay from Berlin in 1927. Rudi (born

1908) followed suit in 1933. Wolfgang (born 1911) resided in Florence from 1933 and later relocated to England in 1939. The eldest, Ernst (born 1903), and the youngest, Victoria (born 1913), were the only ones who remained in Berlin, where they survived the war.

On 10 November 1938, things took an untoward turn. The day after Kristallnacht (The Night of Broken Glass), the Nazi leaders unleashed a series of pogroms against the Jewish population in Germany and recently incorporated territories. This event came to be called Kristallnacht because of the shattered glass that littered the streets after the vandalism and destruction of Jewish-owned businesses, synagogues and homes. The Nazis lined up the Jews in front of the town hall and humiliated them by shouting vile slogans and even spitting on their faces.

Luise, like all the other Jews living in the community, was summoned to the Garmisch-Partenkirchen town hall by the Nazi district leader Johann Hausböck, who informed her that she had forty-eight hours to leave. After being forced to leave Partenkirchen, Luise and Victor spent some time with their daughter in Berlin before managing to cross the border into Switzerland. In Switzerland, they stayed with their family friends in Les Avants, near Montreux. 'It was the most terrible time of insecurity and waiting. When they finally received the immigration visa for India, they travelled to Venice, straight from Switzerland, where they boarded the ship,' shared Flora of her grandparents' ordeal.

On 8 March 1939, the Leyden parents embarked on the ocean liner *S.S. Conte Verde* in Venice for a journey to India that lasted six weeks. 'It belonged to an Italian shipping company that in those years brought many thousands of Jewish refugees from Europe to Shanghai, with a stopover in Bombay.' [30]

On board, Luise found flowers, letters and greetings from relatives and friends, including a farewell note from her daughter Victoria.

> Such a farewell is the hardest thing there is—but from tomorrow we look forward to seeing you again. Even if this day is not yet known, it is certain, it will happen—and probably sooner than we think. And, mamsi, during the time of separation, remember that you are always close to me [...]. You are such an important part of myself that you work across a thousand seas.[31]

Luise documented her time in a diary. 'We finally realise that we must go! We wouldn't survive Hitler's Europe,' she said, and found strength in the words of a farewell letter from a friend, which she quoted: 'Don't follow your own way but follow the way you are guided to.' They followed their path to Bombay, India.

'In this constant uncertainty and instability, I am not able to choose my own way. I must accept that somebody in destiny is guiding me,' she lamented. 'This quote should be my guidance and support me through this period of bitterness. It should keep me open to everything that is beautiful in this world that we come across.'

To her, the majority of people on the ship seemed to be small business owners or entrepreneurs. She noticed families of three generations—grandparents, parents and children—travelling to India, unaware of what the future held. Perhaps they, too, were forging their own paths.

Victor spent much of his time playing chess. The fine chess player found other competent aficionados on the ship. Though Luise's diary notes were filled with the routines of the day, they revealed her constant worry for her children, who were living in different countries.

The ship travelled via the Suez Canal. Luise's notes provide valuable insights into personal anthropology, such as her understanding of her privilege. 'In the evenings we go for dinner to the ship. In normal circumstances, people would come properly dressed for dinner and you'd understand where they come from.

But I am wondering how no one has dressed for such a dinner. No one wore appropriate clothing!' Needless to say, the Leydens came properly attired.

At the Suez Canal, they greeted other ships, even the French ones. In her journal, she talked about the hills and its shapes, the oasis of the palm trees—poison green. The colours and the light were beautiful. It was the most tender yellow, stretching to ochre. These were the colours of the desert sand. Luise slept a lot on the ship, perhaps recovering from all the sleep she had lost out in the past years. 'Life was hell in Nazi Germany,' she wrote.

She attended mass in the ship's church and prayed for peace. While aboard the ship, they received terrifying news from Czechoslovakia. Nazi Germany had occupied the country. This marked a significant conflict, and the Allies had let that happen. She read the newspapers every day and commented on the situation. 'Days full of unrest. I try to paint; I try to write, and nothing can distract me. I look to the ocean. The thoughts are torturing me. I am looking for reuniting with Rudi in Bombay,' she scribbled, anxiously.

The Leyden couple first visited India in 1909 during a world tour, never anticipating that they would return three decades later to repeat the same journey under such dreadful circumstances.

Upon their arrival at Bombay Harbour, they were delighted to be greeted by Rudi, who presented his parents with a bunch of white roses. As they carried their luggage, they were led to 'Mrs. Pimm', Rudi's car. Luise, who had previously been introduced to Mrs. Pimm through pictures and letters, was now meeting her in person. Rudi then drove his parents to Anstee Lodge in Juhu. In her words, 'I am happy that India is accepting us in such a friendly manner. It's a country of my longing from my youth days. It feels like thirty years have never passed.'

✣

Luise (extreme left) enjoying a high tea with her Indian friends and Rudi (extreme right), Albrecht and Victor to his left, at their Pali Hill home

The situation in Bombay was unsettling, but their life was sheltered. In fact, the Leydens' Bombay was antithetical to Hugo Baumgartner's Bombay—the beleaguered protagonist of writer Anita Desai's telling 1988 novel, *Baumgartner's Bombay*. Hugo, a Jewish man who endured the tyranny of the Second World War in Germany and later suffered in internment camps in India, spent his final years wandering the city's streets. He searched for table scraps at tea shops and restaurants, a testament to the city's dark, gritty side revealed through Hugo's story.

In stark contrast, the Leydens' Bombay was anything but unforgiving.

A glimpse into Luise's diary notes confirms this. She described Bombay as 'a poor Europe with its beautiful gardens—bougainvillea of different colours by the ocean.'

In Louis Bromfield's 1939 book, *Night in Bombay*, the American character Bill Wainright made a striking comparison of the two Bombays that existed concurrently. 'Yes, Bombay was fantastic and romantic and extraordinary things happened there, if you didn't notice the coolies, the women and the children sleeping on sidewalks and in gutters as you drove home from a good party about sunrise.'[32]

The Leyden family had become intertwined with the 'fantastic' side of Bombay. The social fabric of 1940s Bombay was a complex weave of class, privilege and tradition. Within this milieu, the British and European communities formed an exclusive layer, hosting elegant soirées and lavish balls that reflected the grandeur of their faraway homelands. Yet, this layer of glamour belied to the daily struggles of the working class, marked by labour strikes and a growing sense of nationalism. Amidst this backdrop, the city's diverse makeup fostered cross-cultural friendships that bridged social divides.

For a while, Rudi's parents lived with him on Warden Road.[33] Their social circle primarily consisted of expatriates, with their house help, Narayan, being the only Indian mentioned in the notes. The parents swam daily at Juhu Beach, and Luise developed a fondness for the dogs near their beachside shack.

While the rest of the city was rationing their food during the war, the Leydens indulged in caviar and oysters at various social gatherings at Malabar Hill. Yet, Rudi's mother was astounded by a particular culinary practice: 'They took the oyster out of the shell. It is uncivilised. You don't do that in Europe. You would never put the flesh out. It's an exclusive food,' she wrote incredulously.

She noted the peculiar fashion choices: 'You can find women dressed in fancy clothes alongside men dressed in pyjamas and sports T-shirts,' she jotted down in her diary.

Rudi's work ethic also drew remarks from his mother, who was unaccustomed to his long hours. 'He's become a workaholic. Since there was a Hindu holiday, Rudi came over at 3 pm, unlike his usual 8 pm!' she noted.

Meanwhile, Victor immersed himself in reading, primarily focusing on Indian literature provided by Wilfrid Russell, a friend of the Leyden brothers. He also devoted time to sculpting with clay and wood and spent hours playing bridge. Their first summer in Bombay was excruciatingly hot. They frequented horse races

Clockwise L to R: The Leyden family of amateur artists — Luise, Victor, Albrecht and Rudi

and often visited the Willingdon Sports Club. There, she observed elegant women in sarees socialising while men enjoyed their drinks on the lawns and played golf.

Bombay was starting to feel much like home. However, a sense of restlessness was growing within them.

At dawn on 1 September 1939, German forces launched a surprise attack on Poland. The news struck a personal chord for the Leydens, as many Germans in India were subsequently interned—the largest camps located in Ahmednagar and Dehradun. Victor was interned at the Ahmednagar camp, but his letters suggested that the experience wasn't overly harsh. He devoted much of his time to reading books and playing chess, but what he missed most were his cigars. Utilising his connections, Rudi approached the Indian Jewish Relief Association, successfully facilitating Victor's release within six weeks. This brought immense relief to his worried wife, who rued the infrequency of his letters and wished for more regular correspondence. These letters have been meticulously preserved by their granddaughter, Flora.

DEOLALI 14.9. 9

DEAREST.

GOT YOUR LETTER of 13.9. TODAY. DON'T TROUBLE ABOUT THINGS, YOU SENT TO AHMEDNAGAR; THEY WILL BE QUITE IN TIME THERE. - I MUST HAVE LOST THE MISSING PIECES DURING THE FIRST NIGHT IN THE HALL, WHEN I WAS LOOKING FOR SOMETHING IN MY BEDDING ROLL. RUDI MIGHT ENQUIRE.

AM VERY GLAD YOU ARE WELL & NOT TOO LONELY.

I AM REALLY QUITE ALLRIGHT, SLEEP WELL, EAT WELL & FEELING QUITE FIT. PLAY CHESS A LOT & READ THE THRILLERS, WHICH I SUPPOSE KAY SENT ALONG. MANY THANKS.

GLAD YOU HEARD FROM LOLLY.

LOVE TO RUDI

YOURS

VICTOR VON LEYDEN

No. 127

Victor von Leyden's letter to his wife Luise, dated 14 September 1939

19 Bombay 25.9.39.Warden Rd. Surve Mansions

Darling.No letter!,the last is dated the19. after your arival.It is hard to be without news,I only hope.that you recieved my letters,Iknow how you would miss them,it is such a helpto have this connection. Yesterday we read in the newspaper of the commitee set up for the release of war internees.So our hopes are very big,that we soon will have you back again. and this awful time of seperation belongs to the pass.Inearly think it was the worst in all these years allthough I know and am persuaded ofthe treatment, gentleman,but a prisoner is a prisonerand to know you go through all that,was and is terrible. So I hope and pray,that our Wiedersehen will be very soon,Dearest.
I spent the sunday with Mily and Sidny at Juhu,Itold you,I got the permission to go there,it is granted up to the first of October.They picked me up at the Brocke bungalow,where Iwas after reporting to the police,Rudi left urly in the morning at 6 O'clock,so I had no car and Mrs Brocke took me to the Police with her car on her way to her reporting place,then I was an hour at that beautiful bungalow till Mollies came.It was alovely day for Juhu,Sidny and I had our bath in the sea,in the evening we had a little walk along the beach lovely light,it was fresh and cool.not to much wind,after the rather trying weather just now in Bombay I felt it very refreshing to have the day out there We were home for a very late tea at 7.Coming home I had my bath,just sat down to read,when my men poured in,Mac and Rudi with him William.They enjoied their day,they saw very pld temples beyond Kalyan,2. cent.B.C.,they say,with the most lovely sculptur one can imagin.Rudi made a sketch from one godess, which he admired very much.They had a bath in the little river,found the country most lovely and green and were happy and thankful to have such lovely day which took their minds a little of all the sorrow and troubles of thispoor world. Now I will write to the boys in London,they will be anxios to have news,Lolly will be in despair,I think he never thought of that you had to go to camp.I must say,departing from the children I realy never thought of war, I never believed that Hitler would dare it,he is absolutly the Antichrist,the more you read in the bible ,the new testament,you realize it,and if he is not destroyed there never will be peace in this world,it will be the end.
This evening Bretts and Goodwins will dine with us,every body whom I see sends his love to you they all asks how you are and think of you.All this kindness and friendship is such a comfort and smoothes down a bit of all the bitterness I wonder how you have passed all these days,if you went in for some sport and games,if you feel well and not more tired.I do hope so.
My best love to you,God bless you and let us hope,that you will be home soon

Yours

Lulu

Luise von Leyden's letter to Victor, dated 25 September 1939

Surprisingly, India is seldom linked with the Jewish exile narrative. Despite hosting a modest number of Jewish refugees, approximately one thousand by the onset of the Second World War, it played a notable role. Bombay, serving as the primary gateway into India, facilitated access under British colonial governance. As a key port city in Asia, alongside Shanghai and Singapore, Bombay was instrumental in welcoming Jews until the late 1930s, marking its significance in this lesser-known chapter of history. Within the Nationalist Congress Party, Jawaharlal Nehru, who would become India's first Prime Minister, responded favourably to the idea of resettling Jews in India. 'The Party remained, however, divided on the issue of Jewish migration,' noted Flora in her essay on Jewish exile in India. 'While Nehru supported selective migration (especially engineers and medical doctors), Gandhi primarily opposed it.'

In India, Jewish exiles received support from the Indian Jewish Relief Association, established by European émigrés in 1934, as well as from members of the Indian Jewish population, including the Sassoon family.

Incidentally, the Langhammers were arrested as enemy aliens by the British authorities after their arrival in India. The couple were interned as prisoners of war, a grim irony given their flight from Austria. They were separated, with Käthe held at Satara and Langhammer in Ahmednagar, where he is believed to have faced hostility from fellow prisoners due to his anti-Nazi stance.

Despite the challenges of internment during the war, Langhammer's commitment to art persisted. Käthe, a woman of elegance and taste, found herself working as a censor for German mail, a position that testified to her commitment to their adopted home.

It was only after Käthe and their mutual friend Rudi submitted newspaper clippings of Langhammer's caricatures of Hitler to the authorities that both were released in 1941.

At *The Times*, several of Rudi's colleagues were called up to serve in the British army. Despite being a British citizen, Rudi, still seen as an ex-enemy alien, faced rejection from the selection board. Yet he continued to lead and manage the team with diligence.

Rudi played a crucial role in conducting the first-ever Readership Survey of *The Times of India* under Frank Coulton's guidance. The team developed a questionnaire distributed with each copy of *The Times of India* and *The Illustrated Weekly of India* on a designated day. A significant number of completed questionnaires were returned. Another team verified and coded them, and tens of thousands of response sheets were recorded on punch cards. The data revealed a noble profile of the publications' readership, with Rudi at the helm of the project.

Advertising work picked up during the war years following an initial decline due to disrupted imports. The British generated a good deal of propaganda material for the Government of India for distribution in the Middle East and elsewhere. Everything else, including the hope for a better world, would naturally arrive once the war was over.

With great fervour, Rudi helped create illustrated pamphlets on India and her war effort, and later the political education of British troops in India. In Rudi's words, '... these were run by a nice and intellectual Captain in the Army Educational Corps, who had liberal ideas and got rapped on the knuckles repeatedly by the higher-up brass.'[34] For Rudi, however, working with him proved to be a gratifying experience, as it imparted a sense of doing something useful. Days turned into nights working on 'Captain Tom's booklets', which had to be written, illustrated, printed and distributed at regular intervals.

During the war years, as Indian manufacturers capitalised on the opportunity created by limited imports, the workload in the department surged. The team handled numerous accounts, many of which evolved into leading Indian advertisers for decades to come. Alongside Langhammer, Rudi contributed to the creation of art calendars, which replaced those previously imported. The team was further strengthened by the addition of Homi Kharas, a Parsi gentleman and copywriter, who eventually ascended to a directorial position at a major Indian advertising agency. With the increasing workload, the team of artists expanded. Importantly, Rudi's bonds with his team members persisted long after they had moved on from *The Times* to explore new opportunities.

The conversations held after hours at his bustling desk gave Rudi insight into his Indian colleagues' dedication to the independence movement. A divergence in priorities emerged: for his Indian colleagues, the primary focus was India's independence, while for Rudi, it was the defeat of Hitler. These were tense times, marked by differing but equally significant goals.

A welcome and humorous diversion from the usual advertising tasks arose with a campaign for a hormone treatment promising to rejuvenate men's vitality. The adverts began in a modest fashion, featuring simple typeset messages like 'Even Maharajas…', subtly implying that the product could benefit even those of royal stature. Surprisingly, the most eager inquiries came from desk-bound bureaucrats in affluent wartime cities such as Delhi and Shimla, which baffled the advertiser. To capitalise on this interest, the advertiser escalated his efforts, commissioning a full-page feature in *The Illustrated Weekly of India*. These elaborately illustrated adverts depicted dashing, uniformed men radiating robust health and showcasing their magnetism in temple settings, much to the delight of young women. Created by artist Ross, the allure of these images was so potent that they not only attracted a surge of orders but also incited controversy among the higher echelons of society. This led Rudi's boss, the managing director, to halt the ads and to adopt a less controversial approach. However, the team couldn't produce an equally captivating alternative, so they reverted to their initial, tamer slogan.[35]

Rudi's services to *The Times* extended beyond his regular tasks. When Japanese submarines were sighted in the Indian Ocean, Rudi served as an Air Raid Precaution (ARP) warden for the employees

Watercolour drawing by Luise von Leyden

at *The Times*, as he was fully trained in the skill. Mr. Turner, an imposing figure with all his bulk and a steel helmet, made for an impressive ARP boss for *The Times of India* building. Rudi was tasked with jumping from the second-floor parapet into the fire brigade's jumping nets—an evacuation procedure, in the event of an air raid. He was often required to repeat this exercise twice—once during the rehearsal and once for the actual demonstration before an assembly of officers and dignitaries.

Rudi left *The Times* in 1944 to take up the position of a publicity manager at a large industrial and trading house, before moving to the Swiss firm Volkart Brothers. However, his close relations with the 'Old Lady of Bori Bunder', whose building is today considered one of the finest examples of Indo-Saracenic architecture in India, continued with the 'Denley' cartoons for *The Illustrated Weekly of India* until 1947. He also regularly contributed art reviews to *The Evening News, The Illustrated Weekly of India* and *The Times of India* well into the 1950s.

By then, Rudi had already established himself as a prominent exponent of art. In fact, the whole Leyden family—referred to as the 'family of accomplished amateurs' in a press article—hosted

Brochure of the exhibition by the Leydens

their inaugural group show at the Bombay Art Society's Salon ('Rampart Row') in 1948. All proceeds from the sale were donated to establish the Artists' Aid Fund Centre. This event featured Albrecht's stunning oil paintings, Victor's wooden sculptures, Luise's painstakingly-done watercolours (taught by Langhammer), and Rudi's political cartoons.

Soon after the grand art show, the Leyden parents left India to return to Germany. Although they looked forward to returning home, they were heartbroken by the wreckage of post-war Germany, and the shock of their oldest son, Ernst, going missing after the Soviet troops entered Berlin in 1945.

In a letter dated 1 October 1945, Luise responded to her daughter Victoria's first letter since the war ended, which she had only recently received. She relayed news of Albrecht and Rudi's whereabouts, commenting on how comfortably the two had settled into life in India.

> My darling,
> It's no dream to reply to your first real letter, which reached us yesterday, it was like a celebration for us... Unfortunately, the deep shadow still lies over all the good that you have said. [...] no news from our beloved Ernst. Yes, the waiting is often unbearable and threatens to wear you down, but then you know that it doesn't lead to anything, on the contrary, patience is the means to get over this waiting time... Father and Rudi often dream about him vividly and then talk about him in the morning, as if they had seen him. Letters work wonders, your loved ones seem very close to me despite your world being so far away. I have your apartment plan that you sent me here with all your letters. I now know exactly how you have arranged yourself with the people staying with you. [...] The terrace with perennials, sunflowers and tomatoes inspired me above all, so I can see that you are still a successful gardener. There is so much in your letter, we have to read it again and again to grasp everything you have experienced and the anxiety about your fate over the years was only justifiable...
>
> Bär [as Albrecht was nicknamed], has become a successful businessman, Rudi, now with a doctorate in geology, works in the art field. Both have British citizenship and are fully integrated into the host country. Bär [...] was successful in these years, just

> like the good Rudi, who is satisfied in his new job at Volkart as advertising manager. He does 100 things —writing his art reviews, articles, cartoons, he does so much, everyone knows him, and he has developed a level of diligence that I have never seen before. His small flat is a centre for a large circle, and he always has artists passing through or their acquaintances stay with him.

In his conversations, Rudi did not urge artists like Ara and Raza to address life's major dilemmas through their work, as he didn't see this as the role of art. Instead, he championed the creation of work that was authentic to their milieu. He believed: 'Every age has its own problems to solve and must work out its own art. For that reason, we feel that any discrimination in favour of a so-called national traditional style would stifle rather than promote the development of good art in India. Good art will in any case speak the idiom of its own time and its own country.'[36]

His role as an art critic allowed him to nurture artists in a different capacity. Rudi's reviews paved the way for many artists, including Raza. He first encountered Raza's work at a rather dark and uninspiring exhibition by the Art Society of India, held at the Cama Hall in Bombay in November 1943. 'I was there to write my critique for my paper and was sorely disappointed by the bad hanging and the mediocrity of most of the exhibits. Then I discovered, tucked away in the darkest corner, a watercolour of Pherozeshah Mehta Road by an unknown artist. I tell you truthfully that my heart and eye took gladly to this little painting,' Rudi declared at the opening of Raza's first solo in Bombay in 1949.[37]

Rudi not only detected the earliest signs of talent in artists, but also helped them with financial resources. Rudi first met Ara when he was working as a car cleaner.[38] Upon realising that Ara was also a painter, Rudi was eager to see his artwork. Lora, as late Austrian collector Eleonore Chowdhury-Haberl was often known, shared, 'To Ara, this was a huge deal because here was a "European bada saab" interested in seeing his work. When Rudi saw how beautifully Ara painted, he bought him material and encouraged him to continue painting.'

In *The Making of Modern Indian Art: The Progressives,* Yashodhara Dalmia noted that Rudi discovered Ara when he was a young struggling artist and offered him a small stipend that took care of all his expenses: 'When Ara tried to return the money to Leyden after making a handsome sum [Rs. 2,000], Leyden promptly refused to accept it and told Ara that he was now on his own as a painter.'[39]

Rudi emerged as a silent voice of reason for the artists. His deep involvement with them likely brought him closer to understanding his own choices: pursuing art instead of geology, and choosing Bombay over Berlin as his home.

CHAPTER THREE

'Don't Mix With These Fellows'

Rudi's influence extended beyond art, shaping not only artistic practices but also personal conduct. Ara, always impeccably suited, gradually embraced a European demeanour, a transformation his foster daughter and writer, Ruxana Pathan, credits to Rudi. 'He was a real mentor and godfather figure to my Inna,' she said.[40]

However, prejudices have a way of creeping in during the most inopportune moments, as they did at an art gathering hosted at Lora's home on Marine Drive in the early 1960s.

Upon a single, squeamish glance at the spare-framed, bespectacled man of short stature and dark complexion, Verghese, the senior waiter at the Bombay Gymkhana, turned to Lora and announced, 'I am not serving this man!'

Ara was a Dalit artist. Lora was aghast. 'He's my guest,' she roared, snatching the tray from him, '—and if you won't serve him, I will!'

In their art-filled drawing room, Lora and her husband, industrialist Bill Chowdhury, hosted some of the city's most elegant art evenings. Regarded as Bombay's first collector couple, they actively promoted the works of artists like Husain, Souza, Gaitonde and Ara. 'Back then, every two months, my husband and I would throw parties for the art collectors and patrons at our home,' Lora recalled during our meeting at her Vienna residence in 2018.

At that party, the city's cultural cognoscenti had gathered. In attendance were art historian and erstwhile Prince of Wales Museum director Dr. Moti Chandra, legal luminary and antique art collector Karl Khandalavala, physicist Professor M. Govind Kumar Menon from Tata Institute of Fundamental Research (TIFR) and Rudi. 'We had four servants, but for thirty people, you needed extra staff. So, I borrowed a waiter from the Bombay Gymkhana. He was handing out little tidbits on his tray, and then he came to Ara. I was standing right there. He said, "I'm not serving this fellow",' she shared, still seemingly appalled by the incident. 'A Christian waiter, probably a convert himself, from Bombay Gym, whom I paid for the evening to serve in my house, refused to serve my guest.'

✣

Born in 1914 in Bolarum, now part of Telangana state, Ara lost his parents at a young age. His mother passed away when he was three, and his father, who was a bus driver and mechanic, died seven years later. However, with the support of a compassionate teacher who discovered his fascination with images and his passion for drawing, Ara—like many before him—came to Bombay in search of a livelihood and an opportunity to immerse himself in art.

> When Ara found out that it costs money to be an art student, he went into service, became a humble hamal (a porter*) in a European household. He went on painting in his own way, till one day he could ask his master, who knew his hobby, to let him off for a few hours every day to learn. He worked in the morning and evenings in a studio, doing object drawings and paintings and even passed a Government Drawing Teacher's Examination. He had an open and quick eye and a skilled hand and learnt well enough what was offered.[41]

Young Ara also spent some time in prison after participating in Mahatma Gandhi's Salt Satyagraha, which was part of India's struggle for independence in 1930. However, according to Rudi, his engagement was more impulsive than a result of political conviction.

After his release, he took up a job as a car washer with a modest salary of Rs. 18 per month working for a Japanese businessman from the Yokohama Corporation. This businessman resided in Sheetal Baug, a sea-facing building in the affluent Bombay neighbourhood of Walkeshwar. Jagmohan, a famed art critic of the time, described Ara's living space as, '... so restricted that it was like a monastic or prison cell. But the paintings that he had stacked in sort of a mezzanine were so many that he showed them one by one, it was a colourful world of his own, of pots and pans, flowers and vases.'[42]

Luckily for Ara, his talent did not go unnoticed. His employers recognised his flair for painting and allowed him to use his spare time to paint at the garage where he lived and worked. They even purchased his artworks, particularly the mythological ones, and encouraged him to submit his drawings to exhibitions. It is rumoured that General Hirota of Japan admired Ara's work and wished to meet him, but the bombing of Pearl Harbour in December 1941 thwarted plans for this meeting.

Exactly a year later, in December 1942, Ara held his first solo show at the Bombay Art Society Salon at Rampart Row. It was inaugurated by C.R. Gerrard, the Director of the Sir J.J. School of Art. The show received substantial mention in *The Times of India*, thanks to Rudi, who wrote:

> ...Mr. Ara is a young Indian self-made artist. He went to no school nor studio but discovered, developed, and advanced his natural talent and passion for painting. Only during the last year did he find it possible to work and live as a whole-time painter. What strikes one first in that one-man show is the enormous productivity and variety of Mr. Ara's brush.[43]

Ara with Rudi

courtesy of Rudi's scrapbook; Gulam Mohammed Sheikh; Asia Art Archive

Rudi's support for Ara wasn't limited to words alone. Whether it was due to Ara's challenging circumstances, his status as a self-taught artist creating remarkable work, or both, Rudi was inspired to encourage friends like nuclear physicist Dr. Homi Bhabha and art patron Hirji Jehangir to purchase Ara's pieces. In Ara's simple, effortlessly composed still life pieces and nudes, Rudi saw 'a pervading sense of naive innocence.'[44]

Rudi's former secretary Katy Soonawalla, added:

> Of all the artists, Rudi was particularly fond of Ara. Rudi felt he had a lot of talent and needed to be supported. He encouraged him to paint and have an exhibition. Ara painted a lot of still life. For years, I did a lot of typing and sent out invitations on Rudi and Ara's behalf. Rudi, once, organised the whole exhibition for him. Each painting at that time was priced at Rs. 100.

In fact, the entire Leyden family, including Rudi's parents, took an active interest in nurturing Ara's talent. They ensured he played a role at the Artists' Aid Fund Centre, which was formally founded in 1950.

When the Leydens established the Fund, they intended to eventually pass leadership to Ara. This transition was initiated during the inaugural meeting of the Artists' Aid Fund Centre on 27 March 1956. Hebbar, the multi-faceted Indian artist, dancer and sculptor known for his portraits and line drawings, was elected chairman, and Gade became joint secretary for the forthcoming year. Two months later, V.V. Oak, who was the honorary secretary of Bombay Art Society Salon, confirmed the autonomy of the Centre. A year later, on 30 December 1957, the word 'Fund' was deleted, and the Centre became known as Artists' Centre. During the 1960s and 1970s, while presiding over the Centre, Ara made it his permanent abode.

> '[By then], the onus of keeping the Centre's torch burning had fallen entirely on his shoulders. With his indomitable spirit with a mission to protect the Centre for the future generation of artists, he initiated fund-raising exhibitions like aiding in 1971 Bangladesh war victims. [Besides], the Centre hosted music concerts, poetry sessions and hobby art workshops. His cultural activities were publicised by art critics of the time. Rajendra Shankar (brother of Pt. Ravi Shankar) used to organise Hindustani Classical music concerts during the weekends at the Centre.[45]

Rudi and Albrecht created a cultural footprint in the city. As Albrecht reflected in a personal essay in 1979:

> When living in India, my brother Rudi and I were always in close contact with art circles [and young artists] in Bombay. There were many of them, and

> Rudi and I encouraged them financially by establishing an Artist's Fund and creating a permanent Art Salon, which was and still is available without any charge or snivel for one-man art exhibitions.

Over the decades, the Centre held several memorable exhibitions, including prints of Albrecht Dürer, the fifteenth-century artist from Germany, and prints by the Renaissance genius, Leonardo da Vinci, organised by the German and Italian consulates, respectively. The venue also featured shows by Ara, Souza, Hebbar and P.T. Reddy, whose work showcased complex compositions, including realistic and expressionistic portraits, still-life pieces and impressionistic landscapes. Similarly, illustrator and muralist Shiavax Chavda displayed dynamic line drawings and paintings that depicted dancers and musicians from India and Southeast Asia.

At the time of completing this book, the Centre was looking for a suitable address to relocate. In December 2019, after losing a long court battle with its original landlord, the present trustees had to vacate the 600-square-foot space in Ador House—previously known as Radia House, and before that, the Sassoon Building. The Centre's trajectory is synonymous with the city's tenacity to keep the old alive in the ever-evolving scape of Kala Ghoda, now dominated by luxury fashion boutiques and fine eateries. 'The Centre used to even have a library, which was accessible to artists like me. We had master modernist Gaitonde as the librarian, too,' said its former honorary secretary and artist Madhusudan Kumar. 'And who can forget Ara's little studio there!'

It was here, Madhusudan recalled, that Husain once recited a couplet to Ara, leaving the artist embarrassed and riled in equal measure:

> *Ara, Ara, Leyden ka pyaara;*
> *Art ho, fart ho;*
> *Matisse ko maara!*[46]

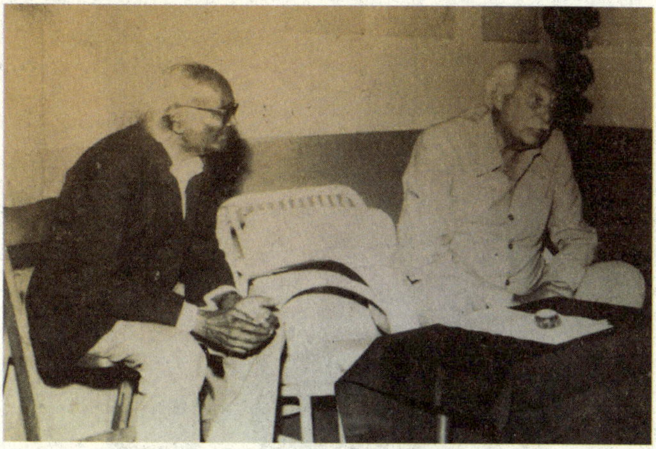

Ara with Rudi in 1982 at Artists' Centre

courtesy of Artists' Centre

Ara, Ara, Leyden's beloved;
Be it pure art, or plain fluff,
It's a Matisse inspiration—let's call out the bluff!

Those familiar with Ara's oeuvre would acknowledge that there is perhaps some merit in Husain's light-hearted jibe.

In those early days, the artist's ideas, though original, were significantly inspired by the notions of European modernism. The French embassy and consulate had a few well-informed individuals aware of the events in Paris, and they shared those influences in Bombay. Painters like Pablo Picasso and Henri Matisse, whose influence predominated in the city at the time, were complemented by the likes of Georges Rouault, Paul Gauguin, Vincent van Gogh, and the German expressionist, Ernst Ludwig Kirchner.

'Ara wouldn't be Ara if he hadn't seen Matisse. We never saw the originals for the longest time. We saw them in books, and Rudi had a lot of literature. Rudi actually said that some of Ara's paintings could really be Matisse's. There's a partial truth in it too. He had a natural love for colour,' Krishen Khanna recalled.

Work by Ara on the cover of the Lalit Kala Akademi catalogue

While Rudi acknowledged that Ara's work was not revolutionary or a significant contributor to contemporary art, he remained personally committed to the artist's journey.[47] He was, according to Rudi, the most direct painter of the Progressive Artists' Group. 'His aesthetics are intuitive and spontaneous, untrammelled by an excess of thought or theory. In that lie his weaknesses but also his great appeal.' [48]

In a 1949 *Times* review of the PAG's Bombay show, Rudi went so far as to compare Ara's large cartoons of card players and beggars to the Dutch master Pieter Bruegel's human realism.

The real secret of Ara's work probably revealed itself to those who engaged with it at length—Rudi certainly did. 'There is no struggle with fate in Ara's painting, no solving of problems; just the pleasure and the pride of painting as a self-sufficient act of life, and as a childhood's dream come true.'[49]

Ara simply adored Rudi and in turn, Rudi considered Ara one of his own. However, Krishen Khanna felt that to Ara, Rudi was always 'sahab'—the European art critic to whom he felt profoundly indebted. 'It's like Ara always maintained that distance from him, Rudi never did,' Krishen Khanna observed.

Rudi's oldest niece Marie-Louise von Leyden nearly welled up as she reminisced about how attached Ara was to Rudi and his first wife, Nena. She recalled celebrating only one Christmas in Bombay, in 1957. Nena had organised an intimate Christmas lunch for the four of them. 'Ara painted a nice picture for me on Christmas and later even took me to a special exhibition, which Rudi wanted me to view because I am also fond of modern art,' she said.

Rudi revelled in Ara's world with mutual respect.

Each Dusshera, Ara would bring out all his work instruments—brushes, paints, easels, canvases, drawing paper and pencil—and perform a little ritual of blessing his tools.

Then a little girl, Ruxana was at the centre of all activities, assigned the auspicious task of putting kumkum (red powder often used in rituals) on Ara's tools. 'Inna was not a believer in any religion, but he believed that there was a supreme being. We used to say our own prayers. His prayers entailed: 'Paintings acchi bikey. Kaam accha ho. Ideas acche aye. Sab khush rahe (May the paintings sell. May the work be good. May we receive good ideas. May everyone be happy),' she said. Rudi too would participate in these rituals at Ara's studio.[50]

⁂

If Rudi was the apparent patron, Albrecht played the role of a silent one. Husain regarded him as the 'Asli Guru (real big master)'.[51]

The other two allies of the Indian art world were Langhammer and Schlesinger. Their commitment to the artistic *métiers* cannot be overlooked. Schlesinger went on to become an important figure in Bombay's art scene in the 1940s and 1950s.

Born in Yugoslavia, Schlesinger grew up in Vienna. He spent much of his early twenties visiting the city's museums and galleries and soon became acquainted with many of the leading artists practising there at the time, including Oskar Kokoschka and Egon Schiele.

Dr. Margit Franz, a historian at the University of Graz, has extensively researched Jewish émigrés who made India their home during the Second World War. Leyden, Langhammer and Schlesinger feature in her German book, *Gateway India*. Her reading suggests that in 1938, Schlesinger's Austrian property was expropriated due to his Jewish background; later that year, he managed to help his family emigrate to the United Kingdom.

> Emanuel Schlesinger himself was able to leave Vienna on 28 February 1939. With the help of a friend, he fled via Switzerland to Italy, where he boarded a passenger ship heading east, with Shanghai as his final destination. But with arrangements of John Klein through the Jewish Relief Association in Bombay, he received a visa for India while on board the ship, and arrived in Bombay on 20 March 1939. In search of entrepreneurial opportunities, Schlesinger concluded an agreement with Messrs. Omprakash Durgadas to start manufacturing pharmaceutical products in collaboration with the Viennese pharmacist Hans Blaskopf (1903–1974). At the beginning of the Second World War, he was briefly interned for two months, first in Deolali and then in Ahmednagar.[52]

During this difficult period, he made the decision to remain in India. In fact, Schlesinger's daughter, Catharine Gonsalves, believed that it was in the internment camp in India that Schlesinger first crossed paths with Langhammer, setting the stage for their subsequent friendship in the art world.

Those in the know about Schlesinger recall his profound interest in Hinduism and Eastern cultures. He later emerged as a significant

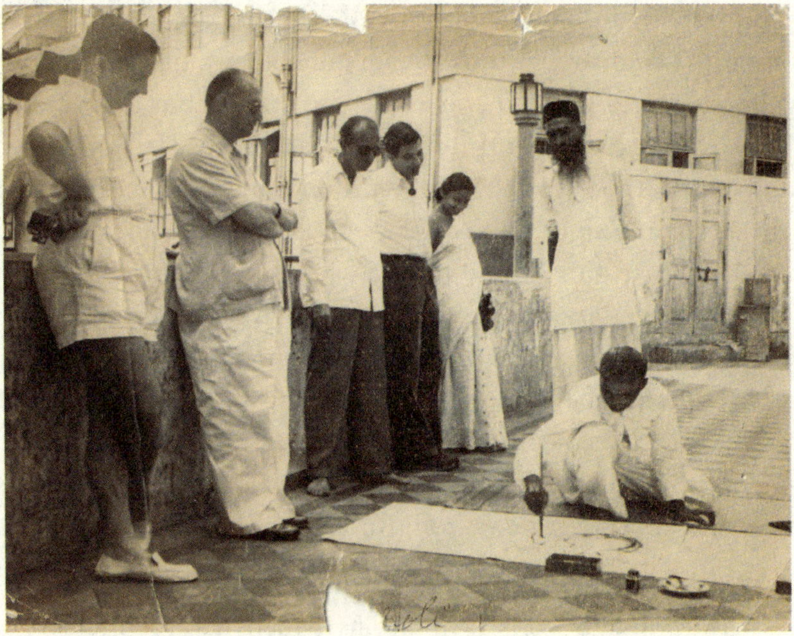

(L to R) Emanuel Schlesinger (with hands folded), Krishen Khanna, Renu Khanna and M.F. Husain watching Ara paint

courtesy of Chemould Archives

patron and supporter of the arts, becoming a familiar presence at art openings of that era. 'Schlesinger not only found a room which became the Bombay Art Society's salon on Rampart Row, but he continually got his friends to buy the paintings.'[53]

Meanwhile, the Langhammers turned their home into a functional art salon. The couple lived on the third floor of an exclusive apartment on Nepean Sea Road, overlooking the sea, and often invited artists over on Sundays to discuss their work. 'Upstairs, one of the rooms had been converted so that they could come there at any time and work. He would show them prints of Picasso, and other masters and dissect their work.'[54]

Langhammer enthusiastically spoke about European art with Indian painters, sharing foreign art periodicals and catalogues. His influence inspired many artists to embark on new ventures in modern art. In an interview with Yashodhara Dalmia, Raza spoke about how Langhammer took to him quite kindly, not only lending him his studio to work in, where he also stayed, but also offering guidance on the type of work he was creating. 'He used to put in front of me paintings by Raphael, El Greco, Monet and Cézanne, paintings of the Persian, Rajput and Mughal miniatures and he would say, "Look at these paintings and tell me what is happening there."'[55]

These conversations prompted Raza to explore different possibilities in art. Langhammer was also an accomplished painter. His portraits unveiled a deep understanding of his subjects, while his bold, explosive bursts of colour reflected the impact of India's light and vibrancy on his artistic sensibility. His initial shows earned him several glowing reviews from Rudi:

> Nothing seems to stimulate his senses as much as the thousand colour vibrations which nature offers to the observing eye in every aspect. Langhammer's paintings come from Kashmir, Shimla, Nasik and Switzerland... The strength of Prof. Langhammer's paintings seems to increase the more he subordinates the visual stimulants of nature to his own sensitive colour imagination and intellectual order.[56]

But Rudi was aware of Langhammer's limitations. In a letter addressed to Krishen Khanna in 1980, Rudi wrote:

> Walter was really two persons in one, a very courageous and honest, upright man who loved his art and was a painter in his eye, his temperament but not his guts. His political ideas were always honest and brave but only Käthe stuck her neck out before and during the early Nazi days. Walter was, in his second personality, frightened and security minded. He wanted the cheque to come in every month and wanted to live without risks. That meant compromises and he finally perished over

> these compromises, which killed his art. Tragic really, and he had paint coming out of his fingers when he wanted.

Unlike Langhammer, who couldn't shake off these conservative beliefs as a mentor, the Progressives demonstrated an incredible appetite for risk. Pundole recollected an anecdote when Husain's senior art compatriot, Narayan Shridhar Bendre, once advised him not to underestimate the security of a full-time job. 'But Husain was quick to dismiss his concern, averring that he had chosen the life of a painter; of that of independence,' said Pundole, whose gallery represented the mercurial painter for many decades.

It is no surprise that Langhammer is remembered more as a mentor to the art world than as a significant painter. In Frank Moraes' words, Langhammer was responsible for building up 'cultural school of painting' in Bombay city.[57]

Kekoo Gandhy, who stood as a devoted mentee, credited his framing business to Langhammer.

In those days, Kekoo Gandhy's business entailed making mouldings for paintings, but Langhammer requested him to make frames. During his interactions, he explained to the patron his vision for Indian art. Kekoo Gandhy shared, 'He believed that contemporary Indian art would have a global impact, similar to the French Impressionist movement. When he said Indian art, he was referring to the various schools—the Bengal school, miniature paintings, the influence of Indian sculpture. India had a great store of inspiration to draw from and the colours and light of India would make the difference, he felt.' [58]

Krishen Khanna made a pertinent observation: 'Langhammer became the great "chachaji of painting" in Bombay. When Langhammer came in, Ara and Raza would get scared, but when Rudi came in, they wouldn't. Rudi could always talk down to the point.'

This endearing quality made Rudi far more affable and less intimidating to many artists, who turned to him for advice, direction in their practice, and even monetary support to keep the

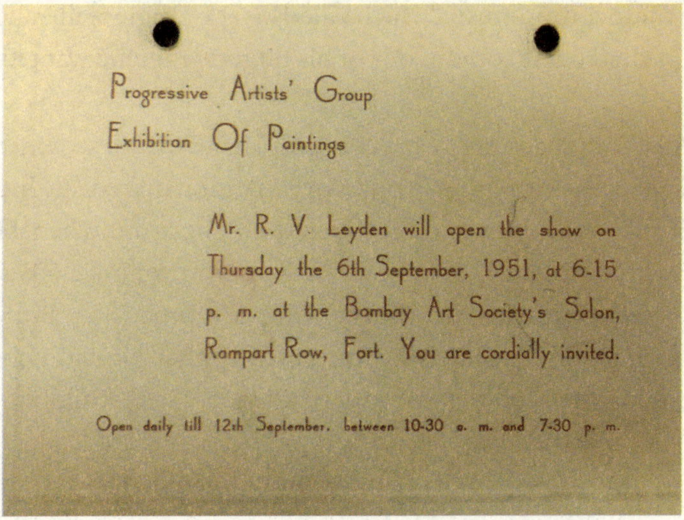
Progressive Artists' Group
Exhibition Of Paintings

Mr. R. V. Leyden will open the show on Thursday the 6th September, 1951, at 6-15 p. m. at the Bombay Art Society's Salon, Rampart Row, Fort. You are cordially invited.

Open daily till 12th September, between 10-30 a. m. and 7-30 p. m.

Rudi was one of PAG's staunchest supporters

courtesy of Artists' Centre

Progressive Artists' Group alive. In a 1948 letter addressed to Raza, Souza mentioned how Rudi had contributed Rs. 100 to the PAG fund, aiding the collective to sustain itself.

Supported primarily by Rudi, Langhammer and Schlesinger, and much like the Progressive Writers' Association (PWA) led by Mulk Raj, the PAG was experimenting to find its own means of self expression. But this new approach to self-expression met with much skepticism. Husain remarked, 'Some of the professors at the J.J. School of Art used to tell the students, "Don't mix with these fellows." They are destroying Indian art. Behind them are three foreigners [Rudi, Langhammer, and Schlesinger], and they are destroying everything.'

And after 'destroying everything', the Langhammers left India in 1957, due to Langhammer's ailing health.

Art patron Sir Cowasji Jehangir presided over a farewell party for the Langhammer couple at the Jehangir Art Gallery. The event was arranged by the Bombay Art Society in cooperation with the Art Society of India, the All-India Women Artists (Bombay), the

(Standing – L to R): Walter Langhammer, K.H. Ara, Emanuel Schlesinger
(Seated – L to R): S.H. Raza, Käthe Langhammer and Rudi von Leyden

courtesy of Artists' Centre

Indian Sculptors' Association, the Commercial Artists' Guild, the Photographic Society of India and the Camera Pictorialists of Bombay, which presented them with a bronze statuette of the Indian goddess Laxmi.

'He was known to the art world as a real, sincere friend,' Sir Cowasji remarked.[59]

Their legacy in the Indian art scene remains indelible. Käthe shared: 'When we left in the morning, we were coming down the steps of the house and there was Ara and [Abdul Aziz] Raiba and they were crying, "Our papa and mama are going ...". It was true and we were touched. I was equally heartbroken.'[60]

Käthe, an elegantly coiffured woman, spent her last years in a retirement home in North London until her death in 1994. In 1981, she returned to India for a visit. Her old place at Nepean Sea Road attracted a group of young artists who eagerly awaited her arrival. Ara was also there, ready to lead her back to the place she once called home.

CHAPTER FOUR

For the Love of Art

Where Käthe Langhammer was integral to the community of artists championed by her husband, Nena—famously 'Mrs von Leyden'—became a cornerstone of Rudi's esteemed cultural circles.

When Rudi met Nena in 1948, he was already an established art critic with *The Times of India* and held a distinguished role as the publicity manager at Volkart Brothers. He occupied a position of authority in relevant social groups in the city, and in Nena, he found the perfect companion to carry on with his earnest pursuits.

'Rudi and Nena were a social couple who complemented each other in every way. She had an equal say in everything he did, outside of work, of course,' shared art historian and environmentalist Dr. Pheroza Godrej, who recalled meeting the couple at her parents' —Mitha and Pheroze Shroff's—many sit-down dinners at their Breach Candy home. Ayaz Peerbhoy, an influential adman and business tycoon, who supported Husain, resided in the same building as the Shroffs, as did Shankar B Palsikar. Known as the mentor of Bombay's contemporary art scene, Palsikar's presence alongside these notable personalities underscored the building's significance in the cultural fabric of the city. Together, they formed quite a cohort. 'They roamed around in a chauffeur-driven car, drank their Scotch, lived a good life but called themselves leftist,' observed Pheroza, then still an impressionable teenager. 'It's funny. I guess, you want to live both lives.'

Rudi and Nena von Leyden

Rudi and Nena married in 1949. A small announcement of their 'Bombay Wedding' even appeared on 6 May 1949, in *The Times of India*:

> Mr. Rudolf von Leyden, son of Mr. and Mrs. Victor von Leyden of Partenkirchen, was married to Baroness Olga Mafalda (Nena) de Belatini, daughter of the late Baron Rudolph de Belatini of Budapest and Baroness Olge de Belatini of Lausanne, in Bombay on Saturday. The marriage was performed according to the Civil Marriages Act, Mr. A.R. von Leyden and Mr. E. Loeffler being witnesses. At a luncheon held after the registration, at the Taj Mahal Hotel, Prof. W. Langhammer proposed the toast of the married couple. A reception was held in the evening at Pali Hill, Bandra.

The reception, which is captured in a black-and-white video now housed at his nephew James von Leyden's residence in East Sussex, was attended by several Bombay residents. The only artist featured in the video was Ara, who was dressed sharply in a suit.

A year before their joyful union, Rudi, who had been involved in a complicated relationship with his former partner, Vera, wrote many fervent letters to his mother about his chance encounter with Nena. These letters, primarily written in German, revealed the development of a passionate connection. Nena had come to India in September 1948 to visit her stepmother, Duzi Bellatini, a painter residing in Mussoorie, a hill station in northern India. Though Rudi and Nena had already forged a cherished companionship, Rudi's heart was still entangled in the past when they met again in December in Delhi, and, subsequently, in early January, when Nena visited Bombay.

Nena, then thirty-eight, was divorced and hailed from a Hungarian family with a German background. The war years had brought immense hardship upon her; she lost her father a year before she set foot in India and, with her mother, fled Budapest in 1944 amidst chaos. Their journey, fraught with challenges, eventually led them to safety in Switzerland. Her mother was a successful portrait painter, and Nena had achieved recognition in Paris for her children's books, which she both authored and illustrated. To sustain herself as an artist, Nena provided art lessons in Germany before pursuing ethnography in Budapest. However, just before completing her doctorate, she had to flee once again.

Rudi and Nena's shared passion for art, ancient Indian monuments and sculptures ignited the initial spark. It was during their conversations about these treasures that they discovered their strikingly similar tastes, values and life philosophies. Rudi seemed enamoured by Nena's charm and intellect, as is evident from the heartfelt letters he wrote to his mother about their growing connection. Rudi's letters revealed the gradual evolution of their friendship into a lasting relationship that spanned fifteen years.

L to R: The Leydens — Marie-Louise with Margit, Albrecht, Rudi and Nena

In one of his letters, Rudi described Nena as 'brunette and about the same size as you, Mams, with delightful colours and a magnificent Borgia nose.' Marie-Louise said, 'When we received a picture of Rudi and her, I remember being impressed with what I saw.'

Almost a decade later, Nena played a crucial role in bringing Marie-Louise to India, expressing a desire to do something special for her after learning of her wartime experiences—her father and Rudi's oldest brother, Ernst, disappeared during the fall of Berlin to the Soviet Red Army in 1945. This gesture marked Marie-Louise's journey to India. Over the next few months in 1957, she split her time between Rudi and Nena's place at Nepean Sea Road and Albrecht and Margit's home in Pali Hill.

In Bombay, she discovered a rather different side to the family dynamic. One evening, Albrecht and his wife Margit organised a party in Marie-Louise's honour and invited several guests. Rudi arrived with Nena, who, on a whim expressed her desire to take Marie-Louise to their place. 'I had nothing packed, nor was I ready. Margit told Nena that she would send for me after a week. This had been arranged before I arrived. They had organised parties where they wanted to introduce me as their niece. But Nena insisted that she would take me then and there. There was a great quarrel between Nena and Margit. Rudi didn't say much. He said, "If she wants it, she wants it."'[61]

The elegant Mithoo Coorlawala, a master's graduate from the University of Cambridge in the late 1930s, was a friend of the Leydens through the art world. She remarked, 'Nena was just very slightly eccentric; she could be odd. She wasn't as warm as Rudi. She liked the people she liked, and not necessarily everybody.'

Rudi's and Nena's partnership was not without its complexities, with both individuals distinct in their personalities and approaches. As Marie-Louise pointed out, 'Rudi was known for his vibrant personality—bright, happy and sociable. Nena, on the other hand, had a more complex disposition. She was always quarrelling with her own mother, and she carried a sense of anger about various issues. Nena was not always easy to get along with. Yet, Rudi was full of love and admiration for Nena, appreciating her artistic talent.'

They frequently collaborated on writing assignments, with Rudi providing written content and Nena contributing illustrations. Their joint efforts included articles for *The Times of India* and *Marg* magazine, where they explored their deep appreciation for art, particularly Indian sculpture and architecture. '[Rudi] was fascinated by the Moslem architecture of Delhi and the North and he considered the sculptures of the cave temples of Elephanta "some of the supreme masterpieces of world art."' [62]

Incidentally, in February 1947, Rudi exhibited fifty photographs of Indian sculpture at the Photographic Society of India. These photos are currently preserved by James, at his home in the UK. The subjects of Rudi's decade-long project included the second-century Sanchi Stupa, the sixteenth-century city of Vijayanagar, and the Mahesh Murti from Elephanta. Rudi's friend Karl Khandalavala, known for his deep passion for ancient Indian art, inaugurated the exhibition.

Rudi felt that to call his humble display a 'photographic exhibition' would be 'presumptuous.' Despite his efforts, Rudi, who lacked technical knowledge and skill, did not consider himself a photographer by any stretch of the imagination. What he intended to show was selected specimens of Indian sculpture, which he found in his more than ten years of travel within India. 'The collection was neither representative of all important monuments or schools nor did it give a historic cross section through the development of the sculptural art in India. It is rather accidental and haphazard in its composition,' Rudi commented on the Indian sculptures, which were subject to temporal, regional and individual styles.

What Rudi felt these imposing sculptures provided was an expression of internal forces of nature through visible form. Through his photographs, he tried to record, not to interpret. In fact, Rudi chose to use the effects of light and shade only as much they were intended by the sculptor.[63] Therefore, as a feature in the *WE* magazine remarked, Rudi's opinions were not mere superficial observations of a visiting foreigner. 'They were based on a fundamental knowledge of art forms, and with the studied appreciation of a scholarly mind.'[64]

Rudi and Nena shared their regard for the architectural marvels with whoever visited them. During Marie-Louise's trip to India, she witnessed the breathtaking beauty of Kashmir with Albrecht and Margit. She also explored the magnificent temples and historical sites in the southern regions of India, including Madras, with Rudi and Nena. The interpretations of these sites often found their way onto Christmas and New Year greeting cards sent to friends and family around the world, in a bid to share a little bit of India with them.

Nena's artistic endeavours extended beyond her travels and partnership with Rudi. She collaborated with author Shakuntala Masani on a book titled *Gautama: The Story of Lord Buddha*,

L to R: Illustration by N.v.L on a greeting card; Nena sketching

published by Macmillan in 1951, where Nena's vivid illustrations breathed life into the narrative. Gieve Patel, who briefly reviewed art exhibitions for *The Times of India* in the mid-1960s, wrote about a posthumous exhibition of Nena's drawings, inspired by Indian sculptures, at Gallery Chemould in 1966. While he praised many aspects of her work, he also noted that her depictions of Indian hips and bosoms did not fully capture the voluptuousness often seen in Indian sculpture.

> A close study of the originals and the sketches shows the workings of a split. There is a certain basic thickness common to all our temple sculpture. Although many of the drawings carry the fleeter limbs of the Greeks, it is remarkable that a fair number have achieved our special bulge of hip and belly, making on the whole for a curious hybrid interest. The heads show up the problem most clearly. Surely Nena has tried to feel her way about a subtle evanescent expression. But drawing after drawing has a head either simple and charming or

(L to R) Portraits of the Coorlawala sisters Asha and Sherena at their Mount Pleasant Road home by Nena von Leyden

> gracefully contented. The crude stone has refused to yield its slow, heavy serenity. [65]

Nena was not only an illustrator; she also dabbled in portraiture. Mithoo, a centenarian, affectionately remembered spending several Sundays at the Leyden home while Nena painted portraits of her two daughters—Asha and Sherena, who were then twelve and ten years old, respectively. They became subjects for Nena's artworks, which, to this day, hang at their home on Mount Pleasant Road, in present-day Mumbai.

Mithoo, who knew about Nena's prolific painting skills, approached her to create these portraits as a birthday gift to her husband Khushroo, who was left wondering where the girls were going every Sunday, wearing the same clothes.

At a makeshift studio in her house, Nena lifted Asha and put her on the table to paint her portrait. Sherena saw a box of colour pencils and grabbed them, and Nena captured that moment in her work.

To keep her daughters entertained, Mithoo, Sunday after Sunday, much to their boredom, repeated the same routine and narrated the same story while Nena patiently created the portraits. 'Unlike my sister, I was shy, and I don't think I fully cooperated. But the funny thing is, during those weeks, I picked up Nena's accent, which I am not sure was Hungarian or German,' Asha chortled.

Although Nena produced a considerable amount of art, she admitted to Krishen Khanna that much of it was intended for sale. The money collected went towards her ailing stepmother's medical treatment. On one occasion, the flamboyant Bal Chhabda, with an unusual parlance—he'd call women 'popdi', men 'geezer', and everything else was 'fatang'—attended a dinner party at Rudi and Nena's home and advised her against doing art solely for financial gain. Bal Chhabda urged Nena to create art for art's sake. 'Nena showed Bal some of her work, mentioning that she was creating it to make money for her mother. Bal being Bal was quite frank with her, and Nena was taken aback by his response,' said Krishen Khanna.

Nena believed that she played an important role in supporting contemporary Indian art. Like Rudi, Nena doted on Ara, whom she looked out for. The much-feted urban planner and architect Charles Correa's aunt Elenor Lobo, was another friend of Nena's. When Elenor's husband José Lobo passed away, Nena suggested to her that she donate her late husband's many suits to Ara. At an exhibition of still-life paintings, which Nena opened at the Bombay Art Society's salon, she described Ara as 'one of the most active spirits of the art life of Bombay.' She found all the seventy-seven still life exhibits displayed at the show to be like 'poems delicately done but with a deep meaning.'[66] Krishen Khanna noticed that Nena displayed a somewhat patronising attitude towards Ara, possibly due to his background, and he would never be able to refute anything Nena said.

Nena was an altruistic person and devoted herself to various charitable causes. She was a member of the Inner Wheel, an organisation closely affiliated with the Rotary Club, currently the

(Standing – L to R): Käthe Langhammer, Rudi with Nena (middle); Walter Langhammer and Ebrahim Alkazi;
(Seated – L to R): Husain, Bakre, Gade, Ara, Souza, Raza and Mulk Raj Anand

largest global women's voluntary service organisation. Her most notable contribution was her involvement with St. Catherine's Home in north Bombay.

In February 1956, Nena headed the Scherezade Ball committee to raise money for St. Catherine's Home. The theme for the evening at the Taj was Arabian Nights and was attended by venerated guests such as industrialist Naval Tata and political leader and diplomat Vijaya Lakshmi Pandit. Nearly eight hundred tickets were sold, which netted a sum of Rs. 35,000 for the Home. 'This charitable work resonated with Rudi, who was proud of his wife's commitment to making a positive impact on the lives of those in need,' Marie-Louise said.

The couple did not have children. Rudi and Nena found their common purpose in art and philanthropic endeavours. It helped that he held a lucrative corporate role, too.

Soon after joining Volkart Brothers in 1944, Rudi firmly established his position as the publicity manager of the company. His vision was clear: to create a comprehensive policy and programme of publicity that would not only boost sales but also help shape the company's image and personality.

Under Rudi's leadership, the publicity department grew exponentially. Armed with just a desk, a telephone, a stenographer, and a budget of one-and-a-half-lakh rupees, Rudi was determined to make a considerable impact. However, as Rudi emphasised, the company's personality was reflected in the personalities of its employees. He believed in the power of effective communication and encouraged everyone in the company to embrace the idea that public relations involved all employees. In his own words, 'Each one of us can also do good public relations in the way he talks of the company and his own work in the company to other people.'[67]

Rudi certainly ensured that the community outside of business was aware of Volkart's support for art. He directed colleagues to buy paintings from young artists of the time. In 1950, when the Indian conglomerate Tata took an internal call to make *Marg* magazine self-sufficient, they decided to devote five pages of the publication to generate advertisement revenue. Tata Sons' Darab Ratanji Dadabhoy Tata personally wrote to Rudi, hoping that Volkart Brothers would advertise with *Marg* in exchange for the highest PR value. Little did Rudi know then that he would cross paths again a few years later with the Tata Group.

A memory that Rudi cherished from his time with Volkart Brothers was a day in the autumn of 1953. Rudi was called to the room of the then-general manager, R. H. Schuepp, to meet with Peter Reinhart, a senior partner of the company. Turning to Rudi, Schuepp enthusiastically said, 'You have done many publicity and promotion campaigns for the company. Here is the biggest and the most vital assignment of your career.' Volkart Brothers was planning to merge the Engineering and Import Divisions into a new company jointly managed and owned by the Tata Group.

Rudi with D.R.D Tata

courtesy of Tata Central Archives

'And it is now up to us to show to our new partners what we are and what we do', he told Rudi, who accepted the challenge.

The ensuing years witnessed Voltas playing an integral role in India's industrial landscape following its formal incorporation on 6 September 1954, in Bombay as a collaboration between Tata Sons and Volkart Brothers.

The 1950s ushered in a period of social change. The city's cosmopolitan allure became more pronounced as it embraced a multitude of influences. Economically, the decade was marked by both aspirations and challenges. Bombay's port continued to be a vital gateway for trade, positioning the city as a hub of commerce. The textile industry maintained its prominence, but there was also an increasing focus on diversification. The establishment of the Bombay Stock Exchange in 1957 signalled the city's intent to play a leading role in India's economic landscape, and the opening of the Indian Institute of Technology (IIT) Bombay in 1958 exemplified the country's commitment to education and technological progress. At that time, the Indian business landscape was evolving rapidly, and companies such as Voltas were looking for innovative ways to enhance sales in the post-war era.

Art patron Lora, who came to India from Vienna in 1957, added: 'When the war was over in 1945, most of the European Jewish people returned home. Only a few returned to Germany because they felt that the atmosphere wouldn't be conducive for them. Fortunately for Rudi, he had a well-paying job here.'

Rudi's professional focus on advertising and publicity made him an influential advocate for standards in Indian advertising. He recognised the importance of promoting these principles on a broader scale, and his initiatives were instrumental in the formation of two key organisations: the Indian Society of Advertisers and the Audit Bureau of Circulations. Founded primarily through Rudi's efforts, these organisations have played pivotal roles in upholding ethical standards in Indian advertising and circulation measurement.

The Ad Club of Bombay, a further testament to Rudi's influence, was inspired by his experiences with the Ad Club of Calcutta. In those days, Calcutta wore the mantle of India's business centre, and Rudi's vision for a similar club in Bombay was realised in 1954. With the support of like-minded individuals, who became eminent names in the advertising industry, such as Soli Talyarkhan, Bobby Sista, Adi Patel, Bal Mundkar and Khurshid Dhondy, the Ad Club of Bombay was established. It aimed to bring advertising agencies and advertisers together, fostering a culture of collaboration and learning. These monthly gatherings, which featured prominent guest speakers discussing key industry topics, became a hub for training and networking in the world of advertising. Five years later, Rudi became the head of the Advertising Council of India.

One project that left a colossal impact on Rudi was Voltas' collaboration with the Kaira District Milk Producers Cooperative Union in Anand in Gujarat state in 1962. This partnership aimed to create a distribution network covering most markets in India for a high-quality, large-volume product line. Voltas, which was already involved in distribution for pharmaceutical producers, sought a product that matched its capabilities. The Amul butter brand had already gained popularity, and their plans to manufacture baby food on a large scale caught their attention.

Rudi visited Anand and was impressed by the scale of the operation, the modern equipment and the spirit of the organisation. He realised that Amul was more than just a business; it was a mission-driven cooperative that empowered farmers and delivered benefits back to the rural communities. In an essay he wrote in July 1982, Rudi looked back on his first meeting with Verghese Kurien, the visionary architect of the Amul Cooperative Movement. Their discussions eventually led to an agreement in which Voltas would handle the distribution of Amul's products.

After one of the closing sessions in Anand, Kurien—better known as the 'Father of the White Revolution' in India—turned to Rudi, and said, 'There is one more river to cross. Our chairman, Shri Tribhuvandas Patel, wants to meet you before we make our final decision.' Cautious about being in the presence of an eminent personality, Rudi went to see the great man alone. Patel had grown up in the vast political movement that gave India its freedom, and he no longer identified as a politician. Rudi was relieved to find out that, unlike many politicians in India, 'he did not possess the overbearing conceit and shallow verbosity that often resulted in ridicule and contempt.'[68]

That same day Kurien informed Rudi that the agreement would go through. Rudi felt that the project's biggest challenge was to build trust in an Indian baby food product, competing against established foreign brands.

Reflecting on the Anand adventure—a collaboration that transformed India's dairy industry—Rudi noted in his 1982 essay the tremendous impact this venture had on rural India. He also highlighted the enduring friendship and partnership he formed with Kurien during this crucial period in his career.

Rudi's job at Voltas gave him immense gratification. He not only received much-needed financial security and a flat at one of the most coveted addresses—first in Colaba, then Nepean Sea Road—in the city, but also the resources to support art and the many charitable causes he attached himself to, especially through his work at the Rotary Club of Bombay. 'Come Tuesday, all the directors at Voltas like Rudi and Paul Gregori left sharp at 1 pm to be at the Taj Ballroom for the weekly Rotary meeting,' said Katy, who was eighteen when she joined Voltas—a year later, she was appointed as Rudi's secretary. Katy also recalled a destitute elderly European woman from a Bombay chawl, who received a monthly small donation from Rudi. 'Later, it became a little tedious for him, he told me to take over the bank account and do it myself. His help would come, I'd write a cheque and he would give it to the woman,' she said.

Now eighty-five, Katy, whose maiden surname was Khajotia, completed a double major in Bachelor of Arts as well as Commerce. She pursued a degree in Law, before marrying into the illustrious Soonawalla family of medical practitioners, whilst working closely with Rudi at Voltas. She recalled the stringent work culture where punctuality was essential. '9 am meant being at work dot at 9 am! That feature about him was very European,' she said. 'But unlike all the other European directors, Rudi never rang the bell to call me in. Instead, he did the typical Indian thing of shouting my name out loud from across the door, "Katyyyyyy!".'

One particularly moving incident for Katy was when she miscarried her second child and was admitted to the Elizabeth Nursing Home, located a few blocks away from Rudi's apartment on Nepean Sea Road. 'Upon learning about it, Rudi visited me at the nursing home. He was my boss, and I was his secretary. He didn't have to come see me,' said an emotional Katy. That's the Rudi she remembers, 'a big man with a big voice and a big heart.'[69]

Katy's tenure at Voltas was filled with memorable moments of fun and camaraderie, such as the secretarial luncheons at the Grand

Hotel in Ballard Estate and the exchange of Christmas gifts. Rudi's thoughtfulness was again evident in the gifts he gave Katy, including a perfume, an alarm clock and even a painting by Langhammer.

Seated in her apartment with one of the rarest Aras taking pride of place in her living room, Katy recounted an incident when one of her three sons, Phiroze—now a well-regarded urologist in Mumbai—met Rudi for the first time. 'Rudi got up and greeted my son with a firm handshake, when suddenly he turned to me and said, "Ma, ah toh giant che (Ma, he's a giant)," and I responded, "Che, pan gentle giant che! (Yes, but he's a gentle giant)."'

How this gentle giant changed the course of Indian art history is something few people fathomed at the time. In fact, Rudi's strong commitment towards Indian art and artists piqued Katy's personal interest in the field. Rudi's cabin at Voltas turned into a makeshift viewing room. During his spare time, artists such as Husain, Ara, Gaitonde and Hebbar—still finding their way in the fledging art world—would drop in to show Rudi their new works, which were modestly priced between Rs. 500 and Rs. 700. He allowed the artists to leave their works in the office in case anyone wished to buy them. And when he did spot a talent, he made it his mission to help the budding artist receive the right training. Rudi discovered Y.K. Kantak, the studio chief of the publicity department of Voltas. When Rudi met Kantak, he was an apprentice mechanic at the Sewri Godown (warehouse), located in the eastern part of Bombay. But he recognised his talent and sent him to art school, and later took him on in the publicity department where he spent thirty-nine years.

Seeing Rudi's unwavering support towards the artists enthused a young Katy to look at art more seriously. 'All the big secretaries at Voltas would get one afternoon off a month. I chose to spend that time going around all the galleries along with my husband [well-known urologist Dr. Fardoon Soonawalla],' said Katy.

Rudi, by this time, wielded considerable influence. When Dr. Bhabha passed away in a horrific plane crash in 1966 in Mont Blanc, the Tata Group released a special volume to pay tribute to his legacy. Rudi wrote about the physicist's artistic side. Besides being an art collector, Dr. Bhabha was an artist in his own right. 'It must have been the last time that I spent an evening with Homi at his beautiful house. As always, the conversation was stimulating and far-ranging, from politics to architecture, from science to art, from food and good cooking to gardening, and there stood, near his desk, an enormous drawing board with huge printed plans pinned to it,' wrote Rudi, of what appeared to be the first layouts for the afforestation schemes and suggested gardens at Trombay, within the area of the Atomic Energy Establishment.[70]

Yet, of all of Dr. Bhabha's pursuits, what resonated with Rudi was how the TIFR became the de facto supreme monument to his artistic vision. As a director, Dr. Bhabha collected the finest contemporary art of its time for the institute.

Rudi was a member of the art committee that played a key role in assisting Dr. Bhabha with the selection of an artist to create a mural for the entrance hall of the institute, a choice determined from the most outstanding of the submitted designs. The competition process ran from the end of 1962 into the first months of 1963. Rudi was joined by Karl Khandalavala, who came to be known as the top legal man working the scandalous Nanavati case in 1959; Phiroza Wadia—Pipsy, Dr. Bhabha's companion; and mathematician Professor K. Chandrasekharan, to determine which artist should be selected. The archival letters at TIFR suggest that many artists including, Ara, Hebbar, Raza, Husain, Gaitonde and Bendre, were approached to submit designs.

Husain's remarkable 45-foot-long mural, *Bharat Bhagya Vidhata*, was eventually chosen from the competition, and today, the mural is considered the single most important work in the TIFR art collection.

Having seen them bloom as artists at close quarters, Rudi felt personally invested in the Progressives' works. He intuitively knew when a work was a product of an instinct, or of a gimmick.

It's perhaps why Rudi wrote a letter to *The Times* when the paper's art critic called Souza's paintings of gargantuan Western females and a lecherous philosopher, 'work of a genius' in 1963. Rudi pointed out that he was not one to be shocked by Souza's exhibition of paintings at the Taj. He had known Souza—and his need to provoke his viewers with his art—for far too long. Although Rudi acknowledged Souza as a brilliant draughtsman who, with his edgy, stabbing lines expressed what he wanted to convey in a few strokes and broke all convention, he was aware of his incongruous meanderings — 'Life was just one big orgasm like my father's,' Souza wrote in his autobiographical essay, 'Life of a Maggot'. Souza's work—featuring women, nudes and his critique of Catholicism—often mirrored his own personality. Although an admirer of his contribution to contemporary art, Rudi, felt the verbiage of praise was unwarranted. His letter to the editor was published in *The Times of India* on 3 April 1963:

> ...Your art critic called Souza's paintings profound and provocative comments on the "human predicament," an indictment of the Western man under the shadow of the mushroom cloud, his first confrontation with genius, and the nonplus-ultra in Indian art, altogether. This may be good for those who according to McColl, absorb their art through their ears, but not for those who went to look. If obsession with oversized and oversexed nudes is a predicament, it can only be that of the artist himself. His many-eyed-and-many-toothed rakshasas whom he calls saints or gods have—probably as much relation to visions of radiation victims as abstract painting has with visions of the atomic structure of matter. Let the artist paint paintings without attributing more to them than he puts into them in the beginning. The violence, in any case, is mostly in the artist's own heart.

> All this does not mean that Souza is not a good painter. Far from it. He is very good and 'The Death of A Pope' is a monumental and great painting by any standards, but let us keep things in proportion and look at the work and not at the words of an efficient public relations machinery.
>
> R.v.L

Souza remained undeterred by Rudi's criticism; he believed he was special and didn't wait for anyone to announce it. He once famously proclaimed, 'John Minton committed suicide because Matisse and Picasso had done everything there's to be done in art. Unfortunately, he had not heard of me, otherwise he would have been alive today.' [71]

London, where he moved to in 1949, goaded Souza's self-confidence further.

The 1950s and 1960s remain the peak periods in his oeuvre, which spanned six decades. After he met his second wife, the British-American Barbara Zinkant, in late 1960s, the couple moved to New York. Souza's marriage with Barbara broke, which caused him great anguish. In addition, America wasn't particularly kind to him, and alcoholism took over. 'And for someone who survived on a lot of ego massaging and praise, it broke him that he didn't receive that kind of attention in New York,' said Pundole, who remained in touch with Souza until the mid-1980s.

Krishen Khanna was almost convinced that Souza, who passed away in 2002, thrived on conflict. 'The thing with Souza was that he was very exacting in his relationships,' he explained. Back in the day, Krishen Khanna aspired to buy Souza's painting, *Autumn Nudes*. 'But it was priced at Rs. 1,600 and I couldn't afford it. I asked if he could reduce the price. He smiled and said, "At 1,600, it becomes your privilege to own it." That was Souza. He gave as good as he got.'

✣

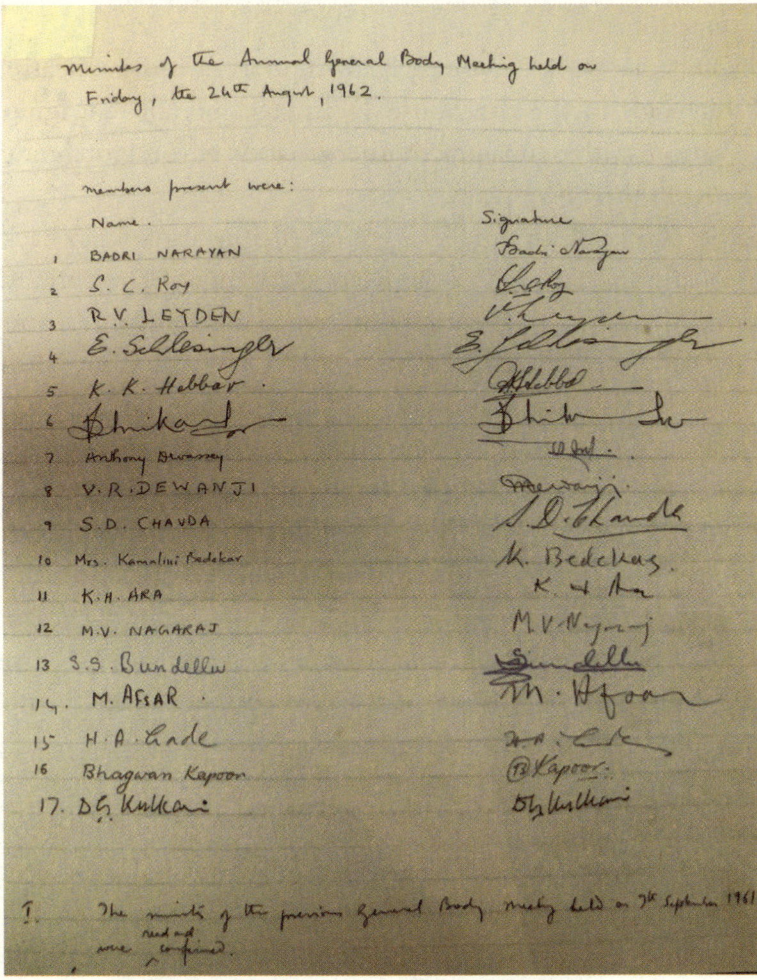

Minutes of the Annual General Body Meeting held on Friday, the 24th August, 1962.

Members present were:

	Name.	Signature
1	BADRI NARAYAN	
2	S. C. Roy	
3	R.V. LEYDEN	
4	E. Schlesinger	
5	K. K. Hebbar.	
6	Bhikan	
7	Anthony Dewassey	
8	V.R. DEWANJI	
9	S.D. CHAVDA	
10	Mrs. Kamalini Bedekar	
11	K.H. ARA	
12	M.V. NAGARAJ	
13	S.S. Bundellu	
14	M. AFSAR.	
15	H.A. Gade	
16	Bhagwan Kapoor	
17	D.G. Kulkarni	

I. The minutes of the previous General Body meeting held on 7th September 1961, were read and confirmed.

Minutes of the 1962 meeting at Artists' Centre, attended by the art community

courtesy of Artists' Centre

Rudi, meanwhile, was delving into the theatrical world. Gieve Patel, whose plays *Mister Behram, Princes* and *Savaksa* grappled with socio-political issues while navigating the complexity of human emotions, aptly described Rudi as a 'Catholic mind' who had large sympathies.

Through his work at Voltas, Rudi supported Indian theatre by publishing ads in their in-house *WE* magazine and engaging in conversations with drama practitioners to look beyond foreign texts and perform their own plays.

In the 1950s, Rudi guided a young Alyque Padamsee, back in Bombay after his training at the Royal Academy of Dramatic Arts, London. Alyque was then entirely engrossed in staging international writing. 'And it was Rudi, who once asked me, why is my Theatre Group Bombay only performing plays by Arthur Miller, Edward Albee, William Shakespeare and Tennessee Williams; why don't we write original plays. That thought stuck in my head,' reflected the late stage veteran, with over seventy productions to his credit, including *Jesus Christ Superstar, Marat/Sade, A Streetcar Named Desire* and *Death of a Salesman*. 'When the opportunity presented itself, I staged a play called *Bandra Saturday Night* in 1961. It had a very Bandra lingo —' What man; bloody bugger'—and created a sensation in the hall. The youngsters clapped at every line, and the old ones were quite offended.'

The production was unremarkable but remained authentic to the social environment. According to Rudi, that was the most crucial element for an artist's growth. He argued that, in post-independence India, the greatest spiritual challenge an artist faced was the problem of orientation. He was particularly concerned about their sense of belonging and challenged the established authorities to facilitate an environment that would inform an artist's practice:

> Where does he belong? Is he of and for the people and must his work descend to the lowest common denominator of public taste and apprehension? Or

> should he be in the *avant-garde* and work for the selected few? Does he really belong to the people in the same way as the medieval artist in India or Europe, who was the herald of his fellows?[72]

Rudi believed great art cannot be confined. Alyque, credited for creating iconic advertisements during his tenure as the chief executive at the advertising agency, Lintas[73], reflected on what these words meant in his seven-decade-long career as a theatre and advertising man. 'There were many art critics writing in English, mainly from England, but they all laid down what is great art. To define anything is to confine. Rudi was a great believer in breaking conventions and not being handcuffed to rules and regulations,' he said.

Alyque took Rudi's counsel into consideration when he chose not to stage playwright Partap Sharma's *The Word,* set in a fallout shelter, in a traditional proscenium setting, but in a theatre that was still under construction. In 1966, the Government Law College in Bombay was building a theatre. It was under construction and had no seating, a space full of dust and concrete. Alyque approached the principal and rented the theatre. 'I got 200 wooden crates for the older audience to sit on. I invited Rudi to the play, and he sat on one of those crates. After the play, he said if his colleagues at Voltas enquired about his awkward walk the following day, he'd say, "Blame the backache on Alyque Padamsee's play!"'[74]

Alyque's closest friend and theatre actor Farrokh Mehta first met with Rudi when he was in his early twenties, working as an advertising officer at Tata, as the company entered a joint venture with the Volkart Brothers. 'Rudi had dropped in to say hello to his great friend and my first boss Farokh Mulla [Tata's legendary publicity director and artist], a passionate supporter of the arts, especially painters,' said Farrokh Mehta. 'When Rudi learned that I was active in theatre, he made it a point to come backstage after every production of Theatre Group Bombay, which I was part of.'

In 1964, Rudi hopped backstage after watching the English adaptation of Girish Karnad's Kannada language play, *Tughlaq*, directed by Alyque, to congratulate the cast. Turning to Farrokh, he said, 'It's nice to see that you're still alive.'

That was Rudi.

'He didn't have to drop by backstage, but he did because for him all the art forms needed to be encouraged,' said Farrokh.

Amal Allana, a theatre director and gallerist, and the daughter of the trailblazing theatre personality Ebrahim Alkazi, remarked, 'Rudi was a man of many interests. He got interested in Alkazi's theatre because he was staging many European plays like Ibsen's and that sparked a friendship.' Alkazi, who founded Theatre Unit from 1950-1962, staged many ground-breaking plays, including Swedish playwright and novelist August Strindberg's volatile *Miss Julie.* Strindberg's play about a wealthy woman having an affair with her domestic help ran into huge controversy. 'This was a bold theme, especially in 1958. Miss Julie was played by actress Alaknanda Samarth and Jean was played by my father. A storm took over Bombay and they were shocked that a "madam" has slept with a male help. There were scathing reviews in the papers,' Amal said.

Alkazi found allies in Shyam Lal, ingenious editor of *The Times of India,* and Rudi, and the trio shared their perspectives in a panel discussion. A transcript of their discussion was later published in Alkazi's *Theatre Unit Bulletin.*

Rudi watched all the productions by Alkazi, who was later appointed as the head of the National School of Drama (NSD) in Delhi in 1962, but he never lavished them with undue flattery. In fact, if he did not enjoy a performance, he was forthright about it. In a review he wrote for the *Theatre Unit Bulletin* in 1961, Rudi was not entirely pleased with Alkazi's rendition of *Oedipus Rex*, the Athenian tragedy by Sophocles. He noted, 'Alkazi acted Shakespeare not Sophocles, but he did it with deep conviction and perfection.'

Rudi and Alkazi also shared a passion for modern art. Alkazi's monumental series of thirteen exhibitions in Bombay in the 1950s, titled *This is Modern Art*, opened a new world of awareness and understanding for the serious student of art and the layperson alike. Rudi even inaugurated one of the exhibitions at Jehangir Art Gallery.

Husain was an artist in whom they shared a common interest. Undoubtedly India's most celebrated painter, who walked around barefoot, Husain was known for his quiet nature, with a preoccupation towards appeasing political heavyweights and high rollers. But both Rudi and Alkazi could look past these idiosyncrasies and acknowledge his genius and the fierce drive that set him apart from the other modern artists.

Rudi described Husain as a 'fauvist painter' and was an early admirer of his works, which were composed with strong colours and bold brushwork. When Husain's 1955 painting *Zameen* met with resistance, it was Rudi who convinced the Lalit Kala Akademi selection committee to acquire the work after some heated campaigning. The sentiment of the panoramic painting, featuring many motifs of India, is 'real, mythical, and symbolic all at once.'[75]

Zameen was considered 'too modern', but Rudi saw merit in it.

In a 1958 letter addressed to Krishen Khanna, Rudi wrote about another of the 'bearded one's magnificent and enormous paintings, *Voices*. I was so impressed by it that I suggested to Alkazi that we do a production of it.'

Rudi and Alkazi collaborated to support Husain's oil on canvas and planned a whole evening at Bombay's vibrant Bhulabhai Desai Memorial Institute (BDMI), where portions of paintings were illuminated, accompanied by a recitation of T.S. Eliot's poetry, 'Wasteland', and music. It was an evening dedicated to appreciating art.

Located in the heart of south Bombay, BDMI served as the ideal venue for the launch of Husain's work. Much like that event, the space was an intersection of interdisciplinary arts. The 1950s were glorious, and one of the foremost cultural hubs happened to be the BDMI, where Rudi was a regular visitor.

The BDMI was founded in 1952 by arts patron Madhuriben Desai, in memory of her father-in-law, the well-known lawyer and freedom fighter Bhulabhai Desai. She delegated the day-to-day functioning of the institute to its trustee-manager Soli Shiavax Batlivala, a friend of her late husband Dhirubhai. Soli, a die-hard Congressman turned card-carrying communist, assisted Madhuriben in transforming the family property into a melting pot of different art forms. Design academic Mahendra Thakkar pointed out in Meher Marfatia's column in the Mumbai-based tabloid *Mid-Day* in 2017:

> Everyone rallied around an ideal of national integration which Solibhai helped put into practice. The country wasn't cut off from a history of art—in Bombay the Opera House and Laxmi Bagh in Girgaon laid the groundwork for such awareness. That underwent a disconnect under the British. But Solibhai walked the talk, ensuring the Bhulabhai represented classicism and modernism in the Indian arts.

The estate comprised two angled bungalows. Madhuriben lived in a road-facing apartment-building, which is now the Dubash residence. The other bungalow was a ground-plus-one Art Deco structure that housed the institute. It buzzed with activity daily from ten in the morning until eleven at night.

It allowed artists of different disciplines to mingle with each other and generate a free flow of ideas. Thespians such as Alkazi and Satyadev Dubey staged plays; danseuse Meenakshi Raja practised her classical dance; sitar maestro Ravi Shankar established Kinnara School of Music in 1962; his contemporary Vilayat Khan, too, was allotted a room, as were sculptors Pilloo Pochkhanawala and B. Vithal. Artists such as Husain, Nalini Malani, Gaitonde, Tyeb Mehta, B. Prabha and Nasreen Mohamedi rented the studio spaces for a nominal fee of one rupee. Gaitonde left Bombay for Delhi in the late 1960s after BDMI closed, citing that India's financial capital had become too expensive for him to sustain a living.

Stage doyenne Vijaya Mehta, who considered herself a product of BDMI, defined this osmotic experience at the space as 'a connection between paint, rhythm and tone.'

The institute was also home to a private art gallery, frequented by Rudi along with Nena. In 1959, Bal Chhabda, a discerning art collector, opened Gallery 59 with a show by Nasreen. Known for her line-based drawings, Nasreen was then a young artist emerging onto the scene. The painters who later exhibited their works at Gallery 59 included S.H. Raza, Ram Kumar, Gaitonde, Husain, Krishen Khanna and Akbar Padamsee. The gallery ended its tenure rather abruptly when Bal Chhabda, also a filmmaker who made *Do Raha* in 1952 with actress Nalini Jaywant, tore down the entire gallery in a fit of rage, after finding dancers practising there. There was rubble everywhere, and the gallery shut thereafter. The bungalow too was eventually demolished in 1969, and a high-storey building, Akash Ganga, was built on the same plot.

As an art student from 1964 to 1969 at Sir J.J. School of Art, Nalini Malani, who in her over 50-year multimedia practice has combined painting, theatre, video and animation to create immersive and politically charged works, was fortunate to have a studio space at BDMI. 'My own studio was next to the big hall facing the garden. On the lawn of the garden, theatre rehearsals would take place. It would be either Alkazi or [Satyadev] Dubey rehearsing for their plays. There was an open-air auditorium on the terrace where Dubey would have his performances. I would help with making invitations by writing and drawing on postcards, making posters and helping backstage,' she remembered. 'Fellow artists such as Gaitonde, Prafulla Joshi (who was an excellent classical vocalist), Tyeb, Bal, Alkazi, Dubey, were all generous with their time. They would lend me their books and argue with me about art and cinema over endless glasses of tea.'

These spirited discussions about the future of art in India would continue at the nearby Swiss café Bombelli's on Breach Candy, where ad and theatre man Gerson da Cunha, along with Alyque, Alkazi, Kersy Katrak (the founder of the legendary MCM, India's first creative ad agency), artist Jehangir Sabavala, and his wife, Shirin, exponent of Bihar School of Yoga, Rudi and Nena would meet. 'It wasn't strictly an art group. Those were interesting times; there was so much happening in the city and there was always something to discuss,' da Cunha said.

✣

Art remained a constant in Rudi and Nena's travels, both in India and abroad.

When he returned to India, after a four-month tour, he spoke about 'What I saw of Art in Europe,' at a meeting held under the auspices of the Bombay Art Society at the Jehangir Art Gallery. In an article published in *The Time of India* on 25 September 1953, Rudi observed that the branch of modern art devoted to abstract art had come to an end in Europe.

> The impetus and tempo had definitely gone out... "There was a swing towards a new kind of realism though the result was not discernible... There is a lull in European art without an attempt to explore new avenues. There is nothing bad in this. For, it is out of such dull periods that great art is born. I feel that a new kind of representational art is coming back, but abstract art will not be as prominent as before," he observed.
>
> "I was struck by the works of the old French artists, but was disappointed with those of the young," he remarked.
>
> Seeing an exhibition of contemporary art in Munich, Rudi said that its output gave one the impression that

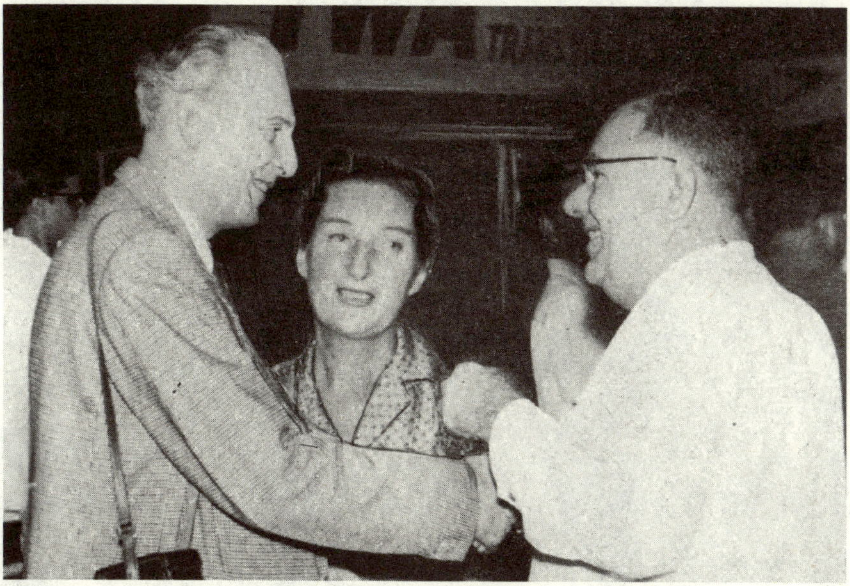

Voltas' R.H. Schuepp seeing off Rudi and Nena as they leave for Europe on a work-cum-holiday trip in the 1950s

courtesy of Tata Central Archives

> it was derivative and imitative, rather than original. "Art in Germany had been suppressed for more than fifteen years, and the artists are imitating what other countries have already done before," he added.
>
> He referred to the Bombay artists who were in Europe, of whom he had met Raza, in Rome, and Laxman Pai in Paris, but not Padamsee nor Souza and said that their stay abroad had not carried them very much beyond what they did before.[76]

In their home filled with state-of-the-art furniture, Nena and Rudi habitually entertained members of art circles. The Leydens would go to plays at BDMI, and on a couple of occasions Rudi invited distinguished people like Kekoo Gandhy, Alkazi, art

India's former Prime Minister Jawaharlal Nehru in conversation with Rudi

collector Jehangir Nicholson, ad men Kersy Katrak, Homi Vakil and Farokh Mulla, an artist in his own right, along with Katy and her husband, back to his house. 'There, they served wine and their staff made the most delicious liver pâté,' recalled Katy.

The conversations at these dinners were not restricted to art. Alyque, who had visited their home on a few occasions described them as, 'cultural stimulators,' where music, theatre and the affairs of the world were discussed with equal enthusiasm.

The couple, members of the Willingdon Sports Club, often swam at the Olympic-sized pool at the Breach Candy Swimming Bath Trust, a favourite pastime. They had a keen interest in music and took pleasure in the melodies played by Mehli Mehta, a renowned violinist and the father of world-famous music conductor Zubin Mehta. They held a special preference for Beethoven's mellifluous music.

The Leydens were well-known among Bombay's elite. 'In fact, when Queen Elizabeth II and Prince Philip toured India in 1961, the Leydens were on a list of select invitees. Albrecht worked closely with the Red Cross in India in the 1930s and was in the first row standing with Margit in her best evening dress. Albrecht was presented to Prince Philip. Rudi went with Nena.' [77]

✣

After he lost his beloved Nena to cancer on 13 July 1964, Rudi took a leave of absence from the social scene. Nena died in Lausanne, Switzerland, where she also sketched her last drawing. 'She was one of those rare persons whose humanity extended beyond sympathy to generous action, for she devoted a large part of her time and energy to the succour of the sick, the forsaken and the downtrodden,' stated an obit note in the *WE* magazine.

A mass was held in her memory at the Cathedral of the Holy Name in Bombay, which was attended by a large gathering of her friends. A choir of girls from St. Catherine's Home sang the hymns of the Requiem.

After Nena's passing, Rudi felt: 'The fire has gone out of the sun.'[78]

'They didn't want to believe it was cancer. Didn't want to make a deal about it. None of us wanted to believe,' said Mithoo, melancholically. 'But after she died, Rudi was devastated.'

A poem penned by Rudi that touched on Nena's cancer ordeal, notes how vastly affected he was by her passing:

For Nena

(1)

Because you came five thousand miles away
And in your eyes the miles shrank to one mile
And lived a little with us where the palm trees sway
And graced the air with your recurring smile.
But left us swiftly on a turning wing,
I raise this small uncertain verse across
The widening seas to chasten and to bless
Not able yet to celebrate or sing
Only set down this record of our loss.

(2)

Now she is dead. But what eternal bonesmith dulled
The dint of brightness on the shallow palm,
The bracelet of these wrists
And the pointed laughter of the still smiling mouth?
And though I need no answer (answer this dead one),
Though she is dead:
What mockery of god took this
Strong affirmation of humanity in flesh
And unchiselled it to dust.

(3)

On a still couch in a still room the body lies.
Someone has marked the eyes indelibly
And shut the strident voice of life. No reply
Goes back to greet the salutation of the street
From an empty room.

How will it be, like this:
The body dark as death and a frail
Dry dust collecting in

Untenanted rooms and bones, Nothing to show
Something once lived, struggled with death and died.

Only this unspectacular last halt
In an empty room?

(4)

I cannot reconcile myself. I am willing to believe
That life itself is quite unreal and death another farce,
But that small human thing in you that drew
Our own humanity and heart, I cannot quite believe
That that has vanished. And so I see them still
Coming to you, the small, the poor, the beaten who despair
Quickening to life beneath your wing, and see you turn
Your face to the brightening air.

— R.v.L

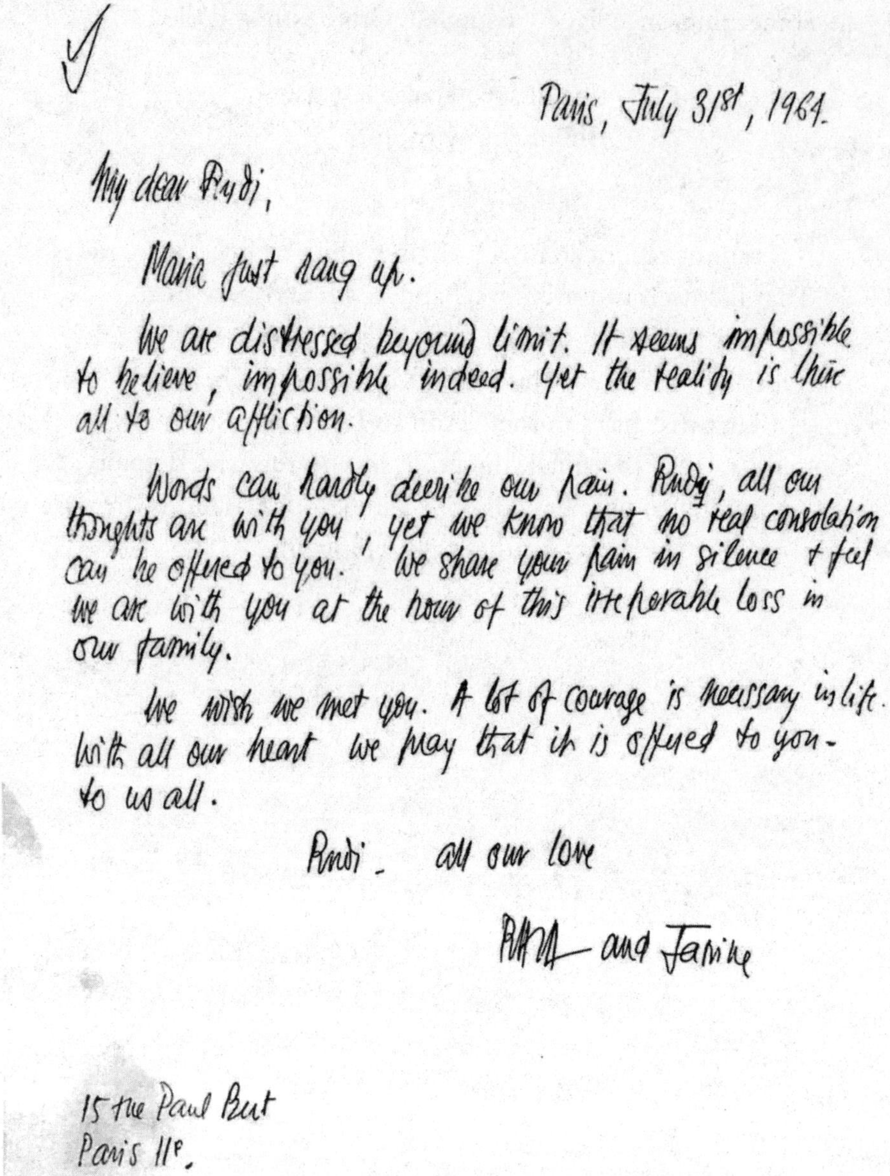

Paris, July 31st, 1964.

My dear Rudi,

Maria just rang up.

We are distressed beyond limit. It seems impossible to believe, impossible indeed. Yet the reality is there all to our affliction.

Words can hardly describe our pain. Rudi, all our thoughts are with you, yet we know that no real consolation can be offered to you. We share your pain in silence & feel we are with you at the hour of this irreparable loss in our family.

We wish we met you. A lot of courage is necessary in life. With all our heart we pray that it is offered to you — to us all.

Rudi — all our love

Raza and Janine

15 rue Paul Bert
Paris 11e.

Raza and Janine's condolence letter to Rudi

courtesy of The Raza Foundation

CHAPTER FIVE

Au Revoir Bombay

The distressing news of Nena's passing reached the artist couple S.H. Raza and Janine Mongillat while they were in Paris. In response to the couple's condolence letters in 1964, Rudi replied:

> My Dear Children,
> Your letter was one of the most beautiful I have received and I feel your love for Nena, her profound sense of loss, your love for her and the utter failure to believe the fact...
>
> Thank you for saying it is a loss in 'our family'. Nena always spoke about you and Janine as 'our children' with all the love of a relative. The pain is still intense, the emptiness vast...
>
> — Rudi[79]

When Flora learnt of Raza's exhibition at The Fine Art Resource, a gallery in her hometown Berlin, she visited the 2003 opening out of curiosity more than interest. She had come across Raza's name in her family archives. 'But when I went up to him and introduced myself as Rudi von Leyden's niece he just looked at me, with tears in his eyes and hugged me,' she said.

An exhibition of Kashmir landscapes by Mr. S. H. Raza, a Bombay artist, was opened by Mr. R. Von Leyden, the well-known art critic at Society's Exhibition Hall in New Delhi. Mr. Leyden is here seen inspecting the exhibits.

courtesy of Rudi's scrapbook; Gulam Mohammed Sheikh; Asia Art Archive

Raza, then eighty-one, was overwhelmed by an inexplicable emotion.

Beyond everything, Raza shared a familial relationship with Rudi, one that transcended the formal association a critic shares with an artist. Hindi-language poet, literary-cultural critic, and activist, Ashok Vajpeyi said: 'Raza would always refer to Rudi von Leyden as one of the three "whoms"; without whom he wouldn't have become the artist that he became in Bombay. There was Schlesinger and Langhammer, also. But the most important was Rudi von Leyden, the critic who discovered his talent.'

When Raza was a twenty-one-year-old artist living in Kalyan, a distant suburb beyond Bombay's periphery, he was exhilarated by the few lines Rudi wrote about his work in a review published in *The Times of India*:

> The 400 pictures that fill the Cama Hall to overflow are a typical cross-section through contemporary Indian art of the last 25 years on this side of India... Many paintings have been shown before and amongst the new ones is no new talent except one or two charming watercolours by a student, S.H. Raza (129), who has a fine sense for composition, and deft colours.[80]

The son of Sayed Mohammed Razi, a forest ranger, and Tahira Begum, Raza spent his childhood near Babaria, Madhya Pradesh, surrounded by the dense forests at the source of the Narmada River, where he developed a fascination for flowers, trees, mountains and clouds.

After completing his schooling from Damoh in Madhya Pradesh, Raza pursued a course at the Nagpur School of Art. Subsequently, he moved to Bombay in 1943, where he lived for seven years. In *Sayed Haider Raza: The Journey of an Iconic Artist*, biographer Yashodhara Dalmia describes the young Raza, dazzled by the metropolis and the overwhelming feeling of earning a livelihood as an artist. Fortunately for Raza, he didn't have to fret for too long as he quickly landed a job as a designer in the Express Block Studios, located on Pherozeshah Mehta Road in south Bombay. Impressed by his sense of dedication and skill, the studios' proprietors, Jalil Sahib and Ashfaq Husain, made him the chief designer.

Raza spent his days working at the office and his evenings attending classes at the Mohan Art Club, headed by M.Y. Kulkarni, a senior artist and a teacher at the Sir J.J. School of Art. Two of Raza's paintings from this period—a street scene from the Express Block Studios and a depiction of a Parsi temple—were selected for the group show at the Bombay Art Society in November 1943. These watercolour paintings, priced at Rs. 40 each—the same as Raza's monthly salary—were the ones that caught Rudi's attention. 'The day after the review [*The Times*] came out, Emanuel

Schlesinger, a generous patron and collector, visited Raza and invited him to Leyden's apartment, where he also met Professor Walter Langhammer,' stated Yashodhara Dalmia.

Rudi had the opportunity of working closely with Raza on a more commercial level in the production of his firm's wall calendars, which were illustrated by the artist for many years.

Rudi saw Raza develop his artistic flair and rapidly grow from strength to strength, winning medals and scholarships. When Raza opened his debut solo in 1949, Rudi was only too pleased to inaugurate the show and make a generous speech. A one-man show is an important event in the life of an artist, especially if it is his first. Rudi compared a beaming Raza to an excited bride on her wedding day or a prima donna on a first night. He was glad that Raza waited over six years to reach a stage of maturity as an artist and present a strong body of work that was befitting a solo. Many artists don't wait for this long, but Raza did. An elated Rudi announced to the attentive crowd:

> What he shows you today, is the work of a balanced, knowing artist, with a personality, with a direction (I avoid the word style), and with the so-necessary experience of nature and art, which springs from years of hard and unrelenting study and work. If any artist worked hard, it was Raza, who spent no idle day in all the years I have known him.

Rudi stated that Raza, inspired by renowned artists Bendre and Langhammer, went through a 'Bendre period'[81] and a 'Langhammer period'. With his debut solo, '... he emerged on his own, and entered his "Raza period", where he handled colour with his own independent skilfulness.'[82]

At twenty-one, when Raza overcame his inhibitions, he primarily painted fluid watercolours depicting landscapes and town scenes. From 1942 to 1944, the city of Bombay captivated the young artist, particularly its vibrant urban imagery. Gradually, his artistic vision broadened.

> The time of transformation came from 1947 to 1948. Study and experience had established confidence and intimate acquaintance with the art of painting. With that came a feeling of independence and freedom from routine and convention. A series of paintings Raza created in Kashmir in 1948 serves as testament to this gradual transmutation of nature, shaped by the artist's own creative will: Raza had entered the 'Age of Adventure' where every day brought new discoveries and new excitements...[83]

During this period, Raza decided to pursue his studies abroad. He began to learn French in anticipation of a French scholarship. In 1950, Raza accepted a painting scholarship at the *École Nationale Supérieure des Beaux-Arts* in Paris. 'Raza Sahab told me when he got a scholarship to study in Paris, Langhammer gave him an overcoat and Rudi a pair of shoes because he could not afford them,' said Ashok Vajpeyi, the current chairperson of The Raza Foundation.

In Paris, Raza was exposed to the paintings of post-impressionists like Paul Cézanne, Paul Gauguin and van Gogh. Influenced by their work, he began to use colour as a construction tool, shifting from gouache and watercolour to more tactile oil-based pigments.

For the first time, he stepped into a world where art was not just taken seriously, but was an intrinsic part of life. In France, the painterly dream seemed within reach, brimming with opportunities. The many art schools, galleries, museums, and exhibitions, frequently featured in newspaper columns, created an ideal environment for Raza to flourish as an artist. 'For someone coming from the artistic wilderness that was India in 1950, the impact was terrific and terrifying.'[84]

Raza travelled to Italy, the southern parts of France and Spain. The landscapes of these countries inspired him, leading to an

Raza with Janine Mongillat

entirely new palette in his work. Vibrant reds and yellows began to appear against looming forces of black and deep Prussian blue on his canvases. Raza found his true artistic calling in France, where he met and lived with his French wife Janine, who was known for her deftly created paintings, sculptures, mixed-media art and installations. Raza lived in Paris until 2010, eight years after Janine passed away.

Between the mid-1950s and mid-1960s, Raza's work was dominated by French landscape scenes, characterised by gestural brushstrokes and a thick application of paint. He had metamorphosed his practice since Rudi first discovered his talent. Through the ebb and flow of life, their friendship endured as did their artistic dialogue. Rudi brought perspective into Raza's technique, discernible in an essay he wrote for the *Sadanga* exhibition catalogue in 1978. The article spoke of how Raza's revisits to India through the sixties and seventies influenced and changed his outlook.

Raza's iconic Bindu from the Sadanga series in 1978

Rudi commented:

> He re-sensitised his perceptiveness for a final supreme and universal viewing of nature, not as appearance, not as spectacle but as an integrated force of life and cosmic growth reflected in every elementary particle and in every fibre of a human being. The five elements which in Hindu thought build this and other worlds—kshiti-earth, jala-water, pawak-fire, gagan-sky and samira-ether—and their correspondence, on the one hand, to areas of consciousness in the human mind and, on the other, to the colours—yellow, padma; white, sulka; red, tejas; blue, nila; and black, krishna captured Raza's imagination to the point of complete identification of himself with his painted work. Nature became to Raza something not to be observed or to be imagined but something to be experienced in the very act of putting paint on canvas.

The iconic Bindus in Raza's work emerged, marking a significant phase in his artistic journey. Art historian Dr. Saryu Doshi, renowned for her expertise in Indian miniature paintings and Jain art, explained:

> To many art lovers, these paintings are infused with a mystical quality in a manner in which he arranges and repeats various forms and motifs. It is akin to meditation or a mantra. To others, they have the beauty of an Indian musical raga, where by improvising the arrangement of the musical note, various nuances are orchestrated in graceful movements.[85]

On Raza's insistence, Rudi agreed to open one of his most important shows in Bern, Switzerland, in 1982. Rashna Imhasly-Gandhy, the daughter of their old friend Kekoo Gandhy, approached Gallery Loeb to organise a show. Although the gallerist acknowledged the paintings' merit there was concern about their potential sales.

'I told her to leave it to me,' Imhasly-Gandhy said. 'Since my husband Bernard was a diplomat, I had the Swiss Embassy behind me. Raza said he would like Rudi to inaugurate the show; he considered him his chief promoter.'

Many of Rudi's contacts from the Volkart Brothers' office in Winterthur attended the opening and bought paintings. 'At the opening, Rudi mentioned how he recognised Raza's talent at a Bombay Art Society show in 1943 and was thrilled to see him shine. His encouragement opened many opportunities for Raza,' said Imhasly-Gandhy.

Throughout the years, Raza remained in contact with Rudi, exchanging numerous letters that have been carefully archived by The Raza Foundation. These letters covered a range of topics, from art practices and travel plans to events in their cities and updates about their personal lives.

✣

Rudi and Lucy Del Marle-Blake on their wedding on 21 May 1966 at Fox Hollow Farm, Downingtown, Pennsylvania, U.S.A.

courtesy of WE magazine, Tata Central Archives

On 5 March 1966, Rudi sent a particularly upbeat note to Raza and Janine. He shared the news of finding love again with a sculptress, Lucy Del Marle-Blake. 'I am going to marry again. I met her here in Bombay when she was passing through and although we had met only for five days, we knew from the first day that fate had meant us to belong to each other.'[86]

After the unfortunate passing of his beloved first wife Nena, this was a moment filled with joy, optimism and renewed hope.

Although Lucy was French, she held American citizenship through her first marriage to Robert Blake, with whom she had a daughter named Anne. Rudi and Lucy got married on 21 May 1966 at Fox Hollow Farm, Downingtown, Pennsylvania, USA.

Shanmil Herzog, a former Bombay resident, was a close friend of Lucy's. Over the years, Lucy became a mentor figure and almost a second mother to Herzog. The Lucy she knew was 'very French'.

'She didn't suffer fools. She was outspoken. Unlike Rudi, she didn't care if she alienated people,' Shanmil Herzog said, over a phone call from Los Angeles.

Lucy, well-connected and a good friend of Gayatri Devi, the Maharani of Jaipur, added a new dimension. Herzog described their dynamic, saying, 'If Rudi was a force in himself, Lucy could be charming when she needed to be.'

A strikingly attractive woman in her mid-fifties, Lucy had many talents. Aside from creating sculptures, she involved herself in many activities during the two years she was in Bombay. Gerson da Cunha, another friend of Herzog's, met Lucy through her.

As a senior in the ad field, da Cunha knew of Rudi when he became an advertising wizard—Rudi received the advertising industry's annual award, ISA-Khatau Gold Medal, in 1966.

In 1961, da Cunha moderated a panel discussion after a luncheon organised by the Advertising Council at the Gulmohur restaurant in Colaba, Bombay, where Rudi participated along with other well-known names within the field including—A.R. Ahmed (Lintas), Masani (Tata) and N. Swaminathan (J Walter).

Rudi was someone da Cunha—the first Indian CEO of Lintas—admired. He was moved when Rudi offered him a place to live. Da Cunha, who had recently returned home to take up his appointment as the deputy head of Lintas after a two-year stint in London, found that the person occupying his flat in New Marine Lines hadn't vacated yet. This person would later become his wife, Uma. In the meantime, Rudi invited him to stay at his Belmonte flat on Nepean Sea Road, where he resided for two weeks.

Rudi continued playing the gracious host to his friends from cultural circles. The few times when Gieve Patel was invited to his house, Rudi hosted poetry readings after dinner. Gieve had published his critically-acclaimed work *How Do You Withstand, Body* in 1966 and was excited to find himself among prominent figures like Kersy Katrak, a well-known ad man; Rajagopal Parthasarathy, a poet, translator, editor and lecturer in English Literature; and

Nissim, the art critic famed for *Night of the Scorpion.* Gieve recited some of his early poems and was met with warm responses, even from Nissim, a man who hardly broke a smile. 'In hindsight, what should it matter to a man who was, perhaps, at that time already in his fifties, what a twenty-five-year-old guy was doing. Yet, he invited me to his home and asked me to read poems amidst all these distinguished poets. It shows his openness,' said Gieve.

Da Cunha thought of Rudi as a 'Renaissance man.' He vividly remembered how Rudi became part of the effort to help Nirmala Niketan College of Home Science with some fundraising activities in 1967. 'And Rudi got me involved. He suggested that we organise a beat music concert to raise money. At that time, the young people were listening to a lot of beat music. I didn't know too much about beat music, nor did the college's nuns,' said da Cunha, also a theatre man known for his community work and civic activism in Bombay.

Rudi was open-minded enough to organise a concert to raise funds, even though his personal preference was Western classical music. Herzog strongly supported the idea; she was convinced that it would capture the imagination of the young. Just days before the concert, disaster struck. The Koynanagar earthquake impacted the Koyna Dam, severely affecting Bombay. A massive power cut followed, compromising the air conditioning at the commodious Shanmukhananda Hall, the venue for the show. Despite these challenges, Rudi insisted that the concert proceed as planned. The show was a huge success; plenty of money was raised from ticket sales and advertisements in the brochure and everybody was pleased, including the audience, the musicians and the authorities at Nirmala Niketan. 'That was the kind of person Rudi von Leyden was. He provided the authoritative environment in which people could ideate and thrive,' da Cunha said.

Herzog added: 'And like Rudi, if Lucy decided to undertake a project, she would give it her 100%.'

Earlier that year, another fundraiser for the College of Home Science was organised. Rudi suggested they host a fashion show where many of Nena's hand-painted saris would be showcased, and Lucy was the natural choice to orchestrate the entire event.

In the past, the fashion show had been organised by the in-house staff and was strictly supervised by the founder principal, a French nun, Colette Galby. Lucy shuddered when Galby introduced her to the potential models, who were selected based on their strong academic performance. Lucy shrieked. After spotting a group of women walking down the stairs, she asked, 'What about those women?'

'They are not doing that well, academically,' Galby replied.

'Am I doing a fashion show or a special class?' she asked, sarcastically.

Herzog recalled the incident with amusement, 'I was there when this argument transpired. Lucy announced that she was going to walk away from the project. It created a real uproar. But because she was Rudi's wife, she won the day and the fashion show was a tremendous success.' Through a fine combination of charm and anger, Lucy persuaded Galby to reconsider.

'If Lucy wanted something, she went out and got it!' Herzog said. 'She did not care whom she rubbed up the wrong way. She always said what she thought.'

✣

In 1967, after twenty-three years of dedicated service, Rudi retired from his position at Voltas. His contributions extended far beyond the expansion of the publicity department; his vision and determination were instrumental in driving significant growth in both the marketing and administration divisions of the company. This was highlighted in an article titled *A Man of Great Stature* in *WE: Hum Sab—The Voltas House Magazine:*

> By the time he relinquished control of these divisions in 1967, they had achieved a remarkable turnover of Rs. 20 crores. This achievement was particularly noteworthy considering that, when Rudi began his

journey with Voltas, the turnover ranged from a mere Rs. 2 to Rs. 6 crores. Through his dedication and strategic acumen, Rudi played a pivotal role in the company's expansion.

Voltas organised two grand farewells—one at their office in Chinchpokli, a far suburb in Bombay, and the other at the sea-facing Sun-n-Sand Hotel in Juhu. At the hotel, many Voltas employees participated in a play written in his honour, titled 'Lawrence of India'. Rudi was given the perfect Indian send-off. His colleagues made him wear a safa (a turban), called in a band to commemorate the occasion, and hosted a traditional aarti. 'However, all this fawning over Rudi was too much for Lucy,' Herzog recounted.

This extreme love-hate relationship that Lucy had with India, where she once expressed in a letter to Rudi that 'the noise was too much,' led to many differences between the two. After Rudi's retirement from Voltas, she decided to move to Paris. Krishen Khanna did not hesitate to speak his mind to Rudi. He was worried that Rudi might feel lonely in Europe. A big part of his life was in Bombay. 'Ara was his find, he was palsy-walsy with Husain, and I was here,' Krishen Khanna said. 'Rudi agreed with me, but he still went; actually, Lucy wanted to go.'

Incidentally, Lucy had already been acting as an official and honorary adviser to the Handicrafts and Handloom Export Corporation of the Government of India, which owned a boutique, Sona, in France. Lucy was hoping to work with an initiative, Aruna, which promoted and sold Indian goods abroad. Though this idea of feeding French boutiques with the best of Indian crafts was endorsed by J.R.D. Tata himself, the prospect of Lucy joining Aruna failed to materialise owing to the tax situation in France.

Upon leaving, Rudi disassembled his entire home and removed all his belongings. Krishen Khanna said, 'Lucy didn't want many things, including the paintings he collected here because she didn't consider them good enough for Paris. She was very assertive.'

A caricature of Rudi by legendary cartoonist R.K. Laxman for the cover of Voltas' inhouse magazine

courtesy of WE magazine, Tata Central Archives

Before finding suitable homes for these paintings, Rudi displayed them at the Artists' Centre. His collection presented the grassroots of contemporary Indian painting. Executed between 1932 and 1967, there were works by Ara, Chavda, Gade, Husain, Krishen Khanna, Raza, Raiba and Souza. On display was Ara's *The Dance*, which was painted by him in 1942; perhaps one of the first work to be exhibited by him. The visitors also got to view the early beginnings of his still-life phase. The *Studio and Flowers* (1950) and the *Black Pot* (1952) served as fine examples.

Souza's *Goa Church* (1947), painted in lustrous colours with a heavy black outline, was striking. The collection also included three of Raza's paintings, two belonging to his pre-Paris period and one painted soon after he went to France. The latter *Mountain Village* (1959), had all the charm of Raza's colourful palette, executed in oils. There was Husain's *Day & Night* (1951); and a Gade, entitled *Omkareshwar* (1948), a landscape in the lush colour scheme for which the artist was well known.

'Special mention must be made of the two canvases by Walter Langhammer. His *Still Life* (1932) is truly a striking piece. Another interesting work is his portrait of Rudi von Leyden, entitled *The Critic* (1943). Going around this exhibition was like meeting old friends. One could not help but be reminded of the days when the gallery was truly the seat of art activities in Bombay as the salon and office of the Bombay Art Society.'[87]

As Rudi was preparing to move to Paris, he left behind a gift for the city of Bombay. He called his friend Karl Khandalvala to express his willingness to donate a painting by Husain from 1951 to the Prince of Wales Museum, now Chhatrapati Shivaji Maharaj Vastu Sangrahalaya (CSMVS), where he was a committee member. At Karl Khandalavala's request, he sent the painting to the Prince of Wales Museum on the same day.

M.F. Husain's "Day & Night"

courtesy of CSMVS Archives

Day & Night became a valuable addition to a separate gallery that they were planning to open, devoted to the development of the Bombay School of Painting, which Rudi did so much to foster. *The Critic* was gifted to the TIFR, a gesture that solidified his association with the institute. It also graces the cover of this volume.

In 1967, a year before Rudi and Lucy, Albrecht and his wife Margit left India. After Albrecht's retirement from the Belgium photography company Agfa Gevaert, they decided to settle down with the Leyden parents at Partenkirchin. As Albrecht, affectionately known as 'Lolly' in the art world, bid farewell to his home of four decades, he extended the opportunity to museum authorities to purchase his artworks. Based on letters found in the museum

Walter Langhammer's "Study of his Mother with a Hound"

courtesy of CSMVS Archives

archives, the founder of the National Centre for the Performing Arts, J.J. Bhabha and Hebbar were co-opted onto the committee responsible for selecting the paintings. The museum committee bought *Bazaar Gate Street* by Raza and *Woman and Child* by Husain on 28 September 1967.

Albrecht donated two paintings to the museum—a Langhammer portrait of Luise von Leyden called, *Study of his Mother with a Hound* and *Studio and Flowers,* a watercolour on paper by Ara.

On the eve of Rudi's departure, the art community bid him tearful goodbyes at many dinners and gatherings. Ara, Kekoo and his wife Khorshed Gandy, hosted a fitting farewell at the Artists' Centre and the Jehangir Art Gallery. To express their gratitude

(Standing – L to R): Hirji Jehangir, Eleonore Chowdhury-Haberl, Karl Khandalavala, Bal Chhabda, Janine Mongillat, Rudi von Leyden, Khorshed Gandhy, K.H. Ara, Lucy Leyden and Amba Sanyal (Seated – L to R): Kabir Bedi, Raza in the middle with Kekoo Gandhy on the extreme right, next to K. K. Hebbar

courtesy of Eleonore Chowdhury-Haberl

for Rudi's tireless service to the arts, it was decided that all the artists who knew him should gift him a self-portrait—a gesture that symbolised how he helped them see themselves.

According to da Cunha, the decision to return to Europe was driven more by practical considerations than personal ones. 'I do think Rudi tried to stay on in India. But he didn't find anything that suited him. When he was at Voltas, he had everything going for him—he had a marvellous flat in Belmonte, a standing in commercial and social circles in Bombay. He wielded an immense amount of power and prestige. He could do pretty much what he wanted,' da Cunha said. 'When he retired, to find a niche of the same kind was difficult by then. That kind of job was now being occupied by Indians. The Indianisation programme had started.'

Rudi came to India on a six-month visit and stayed for thirty-five years. 'I liked the country and its people from the word go, but I now realise that my initial attitudes were very "sahib," and that friendships begin when the "sahib" disappears'.[88]

Artists' Centre farewell for Rudi in 1967

courtesy of Chemould Archives

(L to R) Khorshed Gandhy, Pilloo Mulla, Karl Khandalavala, Rudi, A.A. Almelekar and Nalini Malani (extreme right) at Rudi's farewell in 1967 at Jehangir Art Gallery

courtesy of Chemould Archives

The 'sahib' disappeared very early on for Rudi, who completely immersed himself in India. Lucy, by her own admission, could only handle the colours and chaos of the country in 'small doses'. 'Rudi was Rudi; when I first met him, he was a pipe-smoking European man,' observed Krishen Khanna, who received a family heirloom: a *meerschaum* and a set of seven other pipes from Rudi. 'By the sixties, he'd take his shoes off, put his feet up, just as many of us Indians would. Lucy would nag him about it. I thought she exercised her French etiquette a bit too much.'

✣

In 1968, when Meenakshi Raja was working for a shop of handicrafts and artefacts for the Government of India in Paris, she visited Lucy and Rudi at their home in a suburb called Asnières-sur-Seine. 'He wasn't a friend. I knew him socially as the art critic of *The Times of India*. But I think he was only too happy to see someone from Bombay and so he came to pick me up,' Meenakshi said. 'At the dinner, I found Lucy to be a bit snappy. I only met her that one time and she didn't leave a good impression on me.'

Lucy and Rudi eventually parted ways in May 1968, two years after their wedding.

To Shanmil Herzog, it was a tragedy that the two people she thought so well suited did not get along. 'They both admired each other but I guess he was used to doing things his way. She was equally stubborn,' said Herzog.

In hindsight, Rudi's nephew James felt Lucy was more of a passing fad. 'But he wasn't bitter about it. He was genuinely in love with her. They shared enthusiasm for art, and they had a big appetite for life. It was an equal relationship.'

However, to Flora news of the breakup was expected. 'I had been surprised when he chose to remarry in his fifties and even wrote to him about it!'

Flora celebrated her twenty-first birthday in May 1968, and Rudi came from Vienna to Wiesbaden, near Frankfurt, for the party. However, he had to leave rather suddenly. 'I was at the University in Freiburg at that time. But Rudi had to collect his belongings from the flat in Paris because Lucy and he had broken up. My boyfriend and I decided to accompany him,' Flora said.

May 1968 was a turbulent time in Paris. France was undergoing rapid transformation during this time, fuelled by the post-Second World War baby boom that led to a surge in the youth population. Concurrently, there was growing dissatisfaction with the conservative policies of President Charles de Gaulle, who had held power since 1958.

The scenes in the city were characterised by a palpable sense of discontent that resonated with students and intellectuals alike. Barricades sprang up as students and workers clashed with the police. The sound of sirens and the lingering smell of tear gas filled the streets of the city. Flora added, 'I had a VW Beetle convertible, and my then-boyfriend and I made the decision to drive to Paris amidst all the protests and the rubbish that had piled up on the streets.'

Rudi shared his reactions with his former colleagues at Voltas. 'At first, I was greatly impressed by the spirit of the students, but later angered by their complete lack of organisation and political ideas.' In a brief note in the *WE* magazine, he wrote, 'They are a bunch of confused kids. The result—they got de Gaulle back with more power than ever.'

The turbulent atmosphere in Paris during May 1968 ultimately set the stage for the end of Rudi and Lucy's relationship. Rudi's safe return to Vienna amid the chaos, while collecting his belongings from their Paris flat, marked a bittersweet departure. Their breakup was a complex interplay of personal choices, differences in temperament and changing circumstances. While Lucy continued her life in Paris, Rudi found a new job in Vienna.

Rudi was entrusted with the task of setting up an office for a pharmaceutical and chemical business, Merck, Sharp & Dohme. In a brief note to his former colleagues at Voltas, Rudi wrote, 'I was faced with the most ambitious plan of operations to be done "ekdam" (immediately) upon arrival in Europe. I have been accustomed to this all my life, and to my surprise, I managed to get things ready on the dot. There is still some life left in the old dog.'

CHAPTER SIX

A New Dawn

Rudi celebrated his sixtieth birthday with a momentous move to Vienna. As Rudi settled into his new life away from busy Paris and Bombay, he embraced the tranquil charm of the Austrian city, first in a quiet neighbourhood at Promenadegasse and later at Neuwaldeggerstrasse, located near the Vienna woods.

In India, Rudi enjoyed the privilege of having a house help to run all his mundane chores; in Vienna, he had to cook and clean up himself. But there wasn't much to complain about. He had a car, a fantastic office with a direct view of the opera, a secretary named Ursula, and a new team of eight representatives. 'Rudi enjoyed his time in Vienna. He loved to stroll around the antique stalls and try out all the different food at the Naschmarkt,' recalled Marie-Louise, who visited Rudi in all the three flats he lived in during the fourteen years in the Austrian capital. 'He led a social life and hosted a lot of gatherings in the beautiful houses he set up there.'

In 1979, Krishen Khanna's eldest daughter, Rasika Khanna Mohan, a Bharatnatyam dancer, stayed with Rudi in one of his Vienna residences. She fondly remembered the home's tasteful decor which included numerous paintings, some created by Nena. 'It was quite artistic,' she said of his living space, a testament to his impeccable taste. This space reflected his extensive travels, the convergence of his decades in India with his time in Vienna.

From the opulent Baroque facades of the Belvedere Palace to the intricate Gothic spires of St. Stephen's Cathedral, Vienna's art and architecture weave a rich tapestry of history and beauty. The grandeur of Hofburg Palace and the imperial charm of Schönbrunn Palace showcase the city's regal past, while modern art galleries in the MuseumsQuartier reflect its thriving contemporary creative scene.

Rudi's favourite haunt was the Kunsthistorisches Museum. Its grand façade, adorned with sculptures and majestic columns, sets the tone for the cultural treasures it holds. Nestled in the heart of Vienna, the museum houses an extensive collection of historical artefacts from various periods and regions, including works by famous artists such as Rembrandt, Vermeer and Raphael. One of the highlights of this enormous museum is the Pieter Bruegel the Elder (c. 1525/30-1569) gallery, a treasure trove of Flemish artistry. The museum houses twelve important works by him, considered the world's largest and most important collection of Bruegel's art.

Rudi shared this fascination with every visitor who came to meet him in Vienna. Among these works are Bruegel's masterpiece, *The Hunters in the Snow,* transporting viewers to a crisp winter morning in a remote village, and *The Peasant Wedding,* a depiction of celebration.

In 1968, Geeta Kapur, a senior curator from New Delhi, was pursuing her second MA at the Royal College of Art in London when she made the decision to visit Rudi in Vienna. This visit came about through the recommendation of their mutual friend, Krishen Khanna. She embarked on a journey to Amsterdam, immersing herself in the art of Dutch and Flemish masters, then boarded a night train to Vienna, where she was warmly welcomed into Rudi's home. He drove her around and showed her the great Baroque churches along with every museum there was to see in Vienna. 'We went and saw the Bruegels together,' said Kapur, one of the leading voices in critical art writing in India.

The following year, Rudi took Krishen Khanna on the same pilgrimage. That particular day, the museum gallery exuded an air of serenity, with soft, diffused light bathing the masterpieces in a gentle glow. Udi-Jutta Schneewind, a woman, who was then in her late twenties, happened to be standing there in silent contemplation. Her reverie was interrupted by the much older Rudi, who walked up to her and said: 'We seem to have the same tastes!'

'I was so embarrassed!' exclaimed Krishen Khanna. 'We were in the Bruegel room when suddenly Rudi spotted this young woman. He decided to go up to her and even asked her to join us for lunch.'

Almost five decades later, Udi remembered the day vividly. 'I was a bit flabbergasted,' Udi smiled. 'We laughed a little bit and then chatted. Later, I joined Krishen and Rudi for lunch.'

Before she left, Rudi asked her, 'Where do we meet next Sunday?'

✣

Udi and Rudi's unexpected encounter marked the beginning of an extraordinary friendship that developed over several weeks.

Back then, Udi was living in her hometown of Basel, Switzerland, aiming to complete her education in psychotherapy. With an interest in art, she frequently visited Vienna—a city that, by the late 1960s and early 1970s, was emerging as a hub for artistic expression and experimental endeavours. Throughout the 1970s, the city was a magnet for artists and intellectuals, with its coffee houses serving as hubs where creative minds converged and exchanged ideas. Even the city's theatrical and cinematic scenes thrived, with Vienna's Burgtheater, one of Europe's most prestigious theatres.

For Udi, that day's visit to Vienna was one such cultural odyssey. 'When I met Rudi, I was twenty-nine. He was sixty, over thirty years older than me. Men my age didn't enjoy my passion for arts. We met at the museum and that is a good example of something that we had in common,' said Udi, adding: 'If you share mutual interests, then a life together is easier.'

Rudi's niece Flora Veit-Wild (L) along with his former partner Udi-Jutta Schneewind (R)

courtesy of Udi-Jutta Schneewind

The relationship, however, met with resistance from Rudi's family. 'I don't think his mother was too fond of me. She gave signals that she didn't want to see me in the house,' Udi said. By that time, she had relocated to Vienna to complete her Master's in psychotherapy. 'On her birthdays, Rudi always went to meet her alone at their home in Partenkirchen. But when she visited us, she took a promise from me, "The day you decide you want to marry and have children, you will leave."'

Despite the vast age difference looming over their relationship, Rudi's years with Udi were greatly fulfilling.

Art in all its forms—paintings, sculptures, and classical music—kept Rudi and Udi's lives together. They visited the rich treasures, churches, castles of Austria and travelled extensively across Europe, including Kosovo, Hungary and Italy. 'Life is gentle with us, deceptively so, as the hour of truth will come when Udi

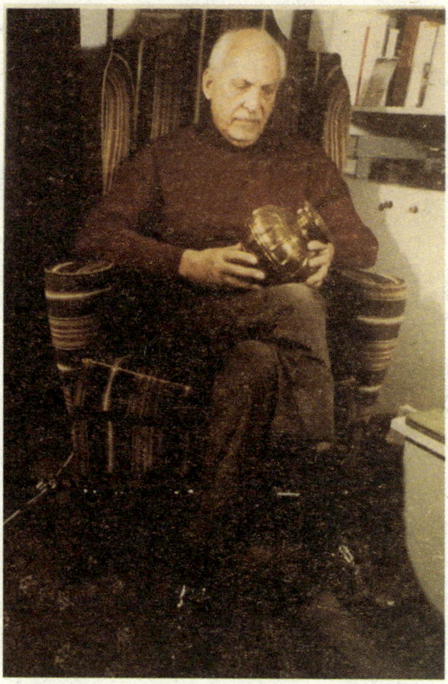

Rudi at his flat in Vienna in the 1970s

courtesy of Udi-Jutta Schneewind

will complete her studies, and I my job, as the reality of a new existence, away from the pleasant and seductive nest of Vienna, will dawn upon us,' he wrote in a letter to Krishen Khanna, dated 2 December 1972.

In 1974, Rudi dashed off another letter to Krishen Khanna and his wife Renu, saying how much he yearned to see them. He mentioned that a new friend was a Sikh man who sold newspapers on the street, with whom he could converse in the meagre remnants of the 'Hindustani' he remembered. He also talked about his ongoing studies in Indian playing cards, which had become the driving force for his upcoming travels to India. Specifically, Rudi needed to translate about fifty pages of Sanskrit text with Kanarese commentary. He expressed frustration that despite reaching out to individuals and institutions in Mysore and Bombay, and offering

Rudi and Udi on their travels in the 1970s

courtesy of Udi-Juta Schneewind

payment, he had received no responses. Even the people at the National Museum in Delhi failed to reply. The only response he got was from his old faithful friend Karl Khandalavala.

In the same letter, he expressed his delight at Krishen Khanna's success in Bombay and enquired:

> Who is buying paintings today? Marvaris as investment or people with some understanding. I would love to see slides or photos of your new figural canvasses. Painting here is dull and I really get more kick out of studying old paintings carefully in order to analyse the ways new vision and new concepts developed in individual painters.[89]

✣

In 1975, Rudi strengthened Austria's relationship with India when he became the president of the Austro-Indian Association, after his retirement from Merck, Sharp & Dohme. He organised concerts, dance performances, lectures, exhibitions and charity events. 'He was even responsible for bringing my guru Kama Deva to perform in Vienna,' said the association's current president, Dr. Radha Anjali, an exponent of Bharatnatyam dance.

In 1979, Rudi was reappointed as the president. That year, Rasika Khanna Mohan was invited to perform in Vienna. She recalled: 'At that time, I had a tour in Europe planned already, so Uncle Rudi, using his good offices, managed to add the Vienna leg. He got fully involved with organising—mic, translation and stage—and was so excited. I stayed in his house for a few days, and he showed me all his beautiful Ganjifa cards and collection of bronzes he managed to source from different parts of India.'

Eleonore Chowdhury-Haberl, who returned to Vienna in 1978, joined the Austro-Indian Association, during his presidency. 'Whenever there was an Indian visitor, he would invite me over to his dinner party. He used to invite people who were interested in the arts. We had the India connection. We knew the same kind of Bombay; the Bombay which was very Westernised,' she said.

Decades later, Lora's oldest daughter, Dr. Martina Esberger Chowdhury, now a mindfulness coach, was invited to join the association. The word that came to her mind when she thought of Rudi was a '*universal gebildet*', a German phrase for someone who is erudite and culturally refined.

Rudi remained drawn to the entire gamut of artistry and craftsmanship of India. In keeping with that spirit, Rudi even organised a fashion show to showcase the best of Indian textiles to an Austrian audience. 'We were a group of young women and he had us pull out sarees from our personal collections and we staged a fashion show—someone wore an Ikat saree, someone a Patola; I wore a beautiful Banarasi,' recalled Martina, with a smile. 'There was no grand budget for this, but Rudi did it with the purest intent.'

As his partner, Udi took an active interest in Rudi's zealous cultural life. The two even travelled together to India. 'I feel grateful that he shared this big part of his life with me. I have made about five journeys to India, since I first visited the country with him,' Udi said.

The year 1977 marked Rudi's first trip to India in a decade. In the second half of the year, he was invited to curate a Ganjifa card-themed calendar for Air India, which usually featured prestigious artworks. Incidentally, when Air India first started producing calendars in the 1950s, Nena contributed images.

For Rudi, this trip was a homecoming of sorts. He was struck by how parts of Bombay now resembled a small Manhattan.

> An enormous euphoria had seized large parts of the electorate after the election defeat of the dictatorial regime of Indira Gandhi. At that time, the masses danced and sang in the streets and squares of the large cities as they did 30 years ago when freedom came overnight... Above all, it was cheered that the hate hunts on men inspired by Sanjay Gandhi had stopped for the purpose of forced sterilisation...[90]

Yet, the prevailing mood that Rudi observed was one of apathy and deep resignation. Nevertheless, he found comfort in the warmth of Indian hospitality and the deep friendships he left behind, which remained unchanged.

During the trip, Udi witnessed the impact that Rudi had made on the cultural landscape of the country when an Air India delegation came to receive him with a great deal of fanfare. 'Rudi was a modest person. In all the years we were together, he didn't make any noise about what he did in India. When I went there with him, I realised what a prominent figure he was; everyone we met was so elated to see him,' said Udi. 'He was busy with making photos for the Air India calendar, but he gave me a reliable guide who showed me around.'

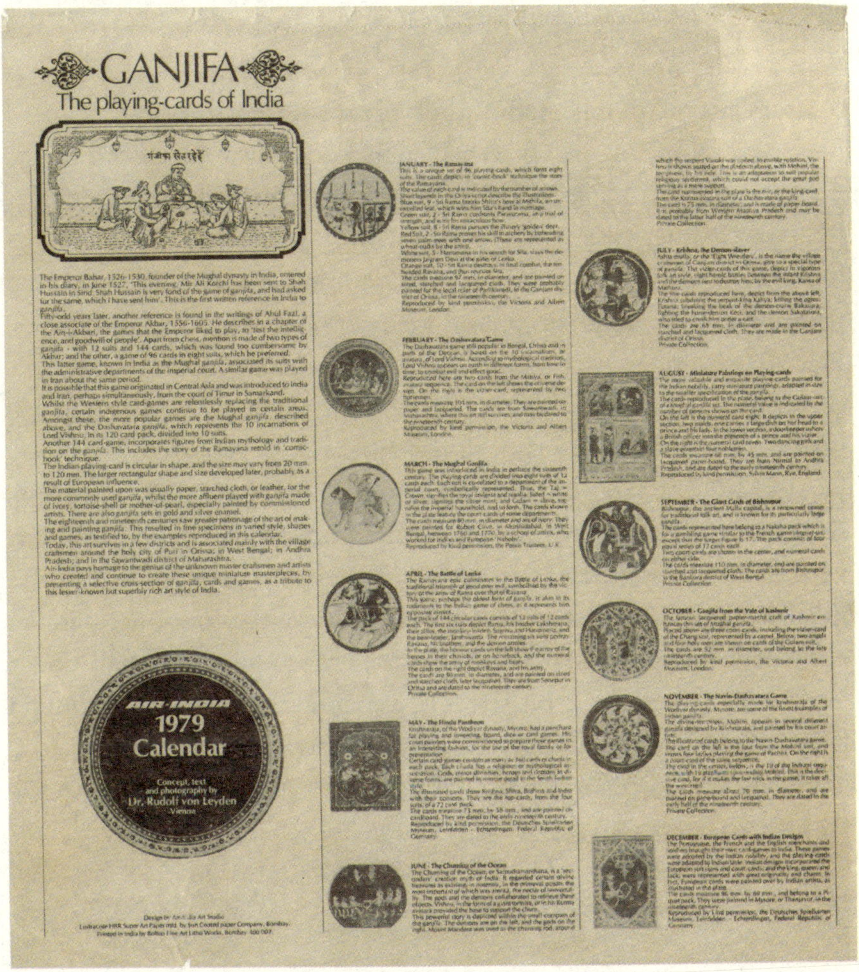

GANJIFA
The playing-cards of India

The Emperor Babar, 1526-1530, founder of the Mughal dynasty in India, entered in his diary, in June 1527, 'This evening, Mir Ali Korchi has been sent to Shah Hussain in Sind. Shah Hussain is very fond of the game of *ganjifa*, and had asked for the same, which I have sent him'. This is the first written reference in India to *ganjifa*.

Fifty-odd years later, another reference is found in the writings of Abul Fazl, a close associate of the Emperor Akbar, 1556-1605. He describes in a chapter of the Ain-i-Akbari, the games that the Emperor liked to play, to 'test the intelligence, and goodwill of people'. Apart from chess, mention is made of two types of *ganjifa* - with 12 suits and 144 cards, which was found too cumbersome by Akbar; and the other, a game of 96 cards in eight suits, which he preferred.

This latter game, known in India as the Mughal *ganjifa*, associated its suits with the administrative departments of the imperial court. A similar game was played in Iran about the same period.

It is possible that this game originated in Central Asia and was introduced to India and Iran, perhaps simultaneously, from the court of Timur in Samarkand.

Whilst the Western style card-games are relentlessly replacing the traditional *ganjifa*, certain indigenous games continue to be played in certain areas. Amongst these, the more popular games are the Mughal *ganjifa*, described above, and the Dashavatara *ganjifa*, which represents the 10 incarnations of Lord Vishnu, in its 120 card pack, divided into 10 suits.

Another 144 card-game, incorporates figures from Indian mythology and tradition on the *ganjifa*. This includes the story of the Ramayana retold in 'comic-book' technique.

The Indian playing-card is circular in shape, and the size may vary from 20 mm to 120 mm. The larger rectangular shape and size developed later, probably as a result of European influence.

The material painted upon was usually paper, starched cloth, or leather, for the more commonly used *ganjifa*, whilst the more affluent played with *ganjifa* made of ivory, tortoise-shell or mother-of-pearl, especially painted by commissioned artists. There are also *ganjifa* sets in gold and silver enamel.

The eighteenth and nineteenth centuries saw greater patronage of the art of making and painting *ganjifa*. This resulted in fine specimens in varied style, shapes and games, as testified to, by the examples reproduced in this calendar.

Today, this art survives in a few districts and is associated mainly with the village craftsmen around the holy city of Puri in Orissa; in West Bengal; in Andhra Pradesh; and in the Sawantwadi district of Maharashtra.

Air-India pays homage to the genius of the unknown master craftsmen and artists who created and continue to create these unique miniature masterpieces, by presenting a selective cross-section of *ganjifa*, cards and games, as a tribute to this lesser-known but superbly rich art style of India.

AIR-INDIA
1979
Calendar

Concept, text and photography by
Dr. Rudolf von Leyden
Vienna

JANUARY - The Ramayana

FEBRUARY - The Dashavatara Game

MARCH - The Mughal Ganjifa

APRIL - The Battle of Lanka

MAY - The Hindu Pantheon

JUNE - The Churning of the Ocean

JULY - Krishna, the Demon-slayer

AUGUST - Miniature Paintings on Playing-cards

SEPTEMBER - The Giant Cards of Bishnupur

OCTOBER - Ganjifa from the Vale of Kashmir

NOVEMBER - The Navin-Dashavatara Game

DECEMBER - European Cards with Indian Designs

Ganjifa card themed calendar for Air India; 1979

courtesy of Tata Central Archives

Following their trip, during which they stayed with Krishen Khanna in his Delhi home, Udi departed for Switzerland to visit her mother. By this time, she had finished her psychotherapy training and was contemplating a potential position in Wuppertal, Germany. One evening, when Rudi came to pick her up, he gazed at Udi and, in that instant, understood the inevitable: 'You are going to leave, aren't you?'

Years later, Udi reflected: 'I didn't leave Rudi for another man—I have never met any man who had such a good heart and who was so generous to me. I left because I wanted to have children.'

A psychotherapist by vocation, Udi is the embodiment of the healer and the seeker, treading the fine line between understanding the human psyche and grappling with her own emotional intricacies. Her aura is tinged with sadness of early loss, having felt the shadow of her father's absence from a tender age—a shadow that perhaps propelled her into the realm of psychotherapy.

After their separation in 1978, a wistful Rudi, then seventy, took some time off and spent the following weeks with Janine and Raza, who by then had settled in Gorbio in the south of France. Even as he absorbed the alluring French countryside, the food, the people, and spent long hours at Raza's large airy studio, in a small house built under trees at the outskirts of a medieval town on a mountain cliff, he yearned for his greatest love—India.

CHAPTER SEVEN

Circling Back in Time

Whenever Rudi thought of India, he thought of Krishen Khanna, and a happy past—a sentiment Rudi shared in a letter addressed to his friend in 1974.

Despite the passing years and the distance between them, the warmth between the two stayed the same. Krishen Khanna was like a younger brother to Rudi, and he considered the Khanna family as his own. He adoringly called Krishen Khanna's three children—Rasika, Malti and Karan—'Rakshasas (monsters)'

'He was like a grandfather figure, my father's friend, but much older. Each time he would come home, he'd bring chocolates and gifts. He would take us out to parks to play and was affectionate towards us,' Rasika Khanna Mohan recalled.

Krishen Khanna and Rudi didn't become friends instantly. 'Our friendship grew over the years. It was given time to grow. It was unprepared, unforced and there was no obligation,' said Krishen Khanna. Perhaps, it was the interconnected past—the trauma of being uprooted from one's home in their early twenties—that cemented the connection. Krishen Khanna was only twenty-two when he witnessed the tumult of Partition and had to leave his home in present-day Pakistan—an experience that influenced many of his works over the years.

Unlike his bond with Ara and Raza, Rudi's friendship with Krishen Khanna was that of an equal. The initial meeting occurred

A young Krishen Khanna (L)
with Nena and Rudi

courtesy of Artists' Centre

in Bombay during the late 1940s. At that time, Krishen Khanna was employed at Grindlays Bank in the city, a position he held for thirteen-and-a-half years. Concurrently, he nurtured his passion for painting, albeit in a somewhat amateur capacity.

Krishen Khanna has described it as a dichotomy—dealing with money all day while spending the nights painting. Encouraged by his artist friends to follow his true calling, Krishen Khanna made the decision to give up his career in banking in 1961, much to the disbelief of his colleagues. This choice was joyously celebrated by Husain, Bal Chhabda and Gaitonde, who, as Krishen Khanna remembered, waited for him at the bank's entrance on the day he resigned. 'It was to welcome me from one life into another,' said the artist, also known for his diverse body of figurative work capturing the vibrant depictions of the bandwallahs, an organised army of musicians who perform at celebratory occasions.

It was during his time at the bank that Krishen Khanna, who had briefly studied art at Lahore's Mayo School of Art, visited the Artists' Centre to learn about developments in Indian contemporary art. 'Rudi and I met each other there a couple of times. I was there in 1948 when his parents exhibited their work; it was a good show,' he recalled.

Rudi invited fellow attendees to his house to celebrate the occasion and asked Krishen Khanna to join them. At that time, Rudi lived in a spacious terrace flat in Colaba, just a few blocks away from Krishen Khanna's residence. Drinks were served and a table laid with cold cuts. A young Krishen Khanna found the entire gathering to be 'quite European!'

When Rudi's mother visited India in 1965 following the loss of her husband, she travelled to Delhi. There, Krishen Khanna drove her to see the Red Fort. To express her gratitude, "Mrs. von Leyden" bought him a little crucible for grinding paints. Rudi brushed off Krishen Khanna's formality and insisted he call his mother 'Mamsi', like him. 'How about you call my mother, "Mamsi", and I call your mother "Mummy",' Rudi declared.

Krishen Khanna's mother was amused by this arrangement. Upon meeting Rudi and being addressed as 'Mummy' by him, she turned to Krishen Khanna and chuckled in chaste Punjabi: 'Aye dekho! Aye medi umar da hain, aur menu ma bulanda hain! (Look at this! He's my age and addressing me as his mother!)'

Krishen Khanna laughed uproariously while recounting the incident. Rudi was permitted to continue calling his mother 'Mummy'. He shared a special bond with the Khannas, who were in every sense—as Lucy pointed out in a letter to Krishen Khanna in 1983—Rudi's 'spiritual family'.

'Years ago, we were taking a ride together in a taxi from Chota Shimla to the city centre, where Daddy was getting off. He embraced Rudi at that stage. En route, Rudi remarked, "Your father is gearing you up to look after the family. A certain sense of responsibility is

Renu and Krishen Khanna

put on you." Rudi was able to pick that up astutely because he was so close,' Krishen Khanna said.

Both Krishen Khanna and Rudi were prolific letter writers. To this day, Krishen Khanna has neatly preserved these handwritten letters in his studio at Gurgaon, a testament to the friendship that still lives on in his heart.

The letters also served as a way for them to catch up on both eventful and mundane activities of life. In one of the correspondences, Rudi mentioned receiving a picture of Krishen Khanna looking rather handsome, but he quipped that he wouldn't share it with him for fear that he might become 'too conceited.'

The correspondence showcases the deep level of trust between the two. In one letter, Rudi expressed how Käthe Langhammer wasn't too pleased with the 'recent Razas' and felt that her husband Walter's art career eventually flattered to deceive. Rudi never mentioned this to anyone else.

In 1968, Krishen Khanna and Prodosh Das Gupta, a significant artist in Bengal's mid-twentieth-century art scene, were appointed commissioners for the Indian section of the first Triennale by the Lalit Kala Akademi. At the same time, Rudi was chosen for the committee of the international award for this event. The Triennale 1968-India, with 620 works from thirty-two countries, became a milestone in Indian modern art history. In what turned out to be his last piece for *The Times of India* before leaving India in 1968, Rudi wrote about the Triennale. He described it as 'not only a worthwhile attempt but a success of considerable dimensions.'

The American artist Joseph Cornell's *Boxes* was awarded the gold medal in sculpture. The artist's use of small boxes to create simple compositions was intriguing to the committee. 'It was quite playful, yet quite serious. Painting was considered art at that time—that was a credo. But the high-powered committee wanted to give the *Boxes* the award,' said Krishen Khanna, who learnt of the committee's behind-the-scenes discussions from Rudi.

In one of his letters, Rudi asked about Krishen Khanna's recent art projects and mentioned that his former partner, Lucy, was greatly impressed. After their separation, Lucy and Rudi had maintained a friendship, which included a joint trip to Yugoslavia to admire the medieval frescoes in the monasteries. Their bond reignited in 1981, leading to them travelling together to India the following year. During this visit, they spent a significant amount of time with Krishen Khanna and his family. 'They told me my house is very lucky for them,' he laughed.

Rudi harboured the ambition to showcase contemporary art on an international stage, a dream he shared with Krishen Khanna and Kekoo Gandhy. While Kekoo Gandhy strived to represent the

Rudi's portrait by Husain

artists at Winterthur Museum in Switzerland, contemplating an exhibition entitled 'Search of Identity of Indian Painter' in 1977, Rudi discussed with the German director of a new Museum of Modern Art the possibility of hosting an Indian art show. Rudi succeeded in presenting a few catalogues and slides to the director, sparking his interest. This led the director to consider approaching the government for funding. Rudi was hopeful of accompanying the director on a trip to India to meet the artists.

As the president of the Austro-Indian Association, Rudi played a key role in facilitating individual art shows. They included assisting Husain in exhibiting his work at Gallery 10 in Vienna in 1981, where Husain exhibited his seminal Mother Teresa series. 'Though the show was a success, Rudi mentioned to me Husain was the kind of person who really wanted major arrangements made for him. So in the process, all the people flocked to the drinks that were served and left the art on its own,' said Krishen Khanna, who visited Rudi that same year and travelled around Europe.

During one of my numerous meetings with Krishen Khanna, his wife Renu, joined the conversation: 'Rudi was a great influence on us, and he knew a lot. So, from him we could get guidance to what we read and what we understood in art in general. We enjoyed his enthusiasm.'

They enjoyed his passion for Ganjifa cards too, even if they didn't always fully understand it.

✣

Rudi's obsession with the Ganjifa cards wasn't a hobby he picked up post-retirement. On a Saturday afternoon in 1939, Rudi was wandering through Chor Bazaar in Bombay. This market, renowned for its second-hand goods and antiques, is where he found a small, colourful box. Inside it were round painted cards made of cardboard. 'I did not know what they represented, but I liked them and so I took home my first set of Ganjifa playing cards,' he recalled.[91] In fact, Rudi was so intrigued that he researched and wrote an in-depth article in *The Illustrated Weekly of India*.

These magnificently crafted cards have a rich history that spans continents, cultures and dynasties. Ganjifa cards, also known as Ganjifeh, Ganjapa, or Gânjaphâ, have their roots embedded in the cultural tapestry of ancient India. The word 'Ganjifa' is believed to be derived from the Persian term 'Ganjifeh,' which means 'treasure cards'. The cards have their origins in the Mughal era, dating back to the sixteenth century.

The earliest Ganjifa cards were used as entertainment but were also intricately designed, adorned with symbols, motifs and themes. Often hand-painted on materials such as ivory, wood, or palm leaves, each set was a work of art.

Rudi organised the Ganjifa art show in Vienna in 1982

One aspect of Ganjifa cards that captivated Rudi was their unique structure. Unlike the standard deck of fifty-two playing cards common in contemporary card games, Ganjifa card decks typically range from ninety-six to 144 in number. For instance, the popular Dashavatara Ganjifa consists of 120 cards, divided into ten suits of twelve cards each. These cards each feature distinct symbols and designs. The number of suits and their specific symbols can differ, reflecting the regional traditions of Ganjifa cards.

Some common games include: (i) Dashavatara, which depicts as King of each suit of the ten incarnations of Lord Vishnu; (ii) Navagraha, representing the nine celestial bodies of Hindu astrology; (iii) Ashta Malla, displaying eight cards with warriors, animals, or other objects and (iv) Rupavati, representing courtly figures.

Gwenael Beuchet, Attaché de Conservation du Patrimoine, in Paris, says, 'The Mughal Ganjifa is the original model in India, with eight suits of twelve cards illustrating the different services of the royal court: the court itself, the treasure, the army, gold and silver coins, the servants, the harem or zenana, the merchants as well as the administration.'

Ganjifa cards, gradually spread to various regions of India, such as Rajasthan, Odisha, the Deccan and Karnataka. As they moved across regions, the cards began to adopt regional characteristics and designs.

Initially, Krishen Khanna was dismissive of Rudi's obsession with Ganjifas. 'To some of us who don't play cards, Ganjifa is a silly exercise and a complex game,' Krishen Khanna said. 'Some of these cards were good to look at. I thought it was a bit quirky. But Rudi was interested in the way these cards are made and became a compulsive collector.'

Krishen Khanna's bemusement at Rudi's new-found interest changed after he heard him speak lucidly about Ganjifa at the India International Centre in Delhi.

Rudi von Leyden is now considered one of the leading experts in this field. 'I am satisfied that India gave me this very minor but, for me, important passion of doing the first complete survey of Ganjifa. It is a facet of Indian life which people like to sweep under the carpet because gambling is "not nice". But that artists made the most wonderful small masterpieces for this "vice" nobody wants to see,' Rudi said.

His journey into the world of Ganjifa cards was driven by a desire to disseminate knowledge about these cards to a wider audience. He did this through the comprehensive catalogues he wrote for the Victoria and Albert Museum in London and the Museum für Völkerkunde in Vienna and the Deutsches Spielkartenmuseum [*Indische Spielkarten*, 1977], as well as within the International Playing Card Society, of which he became president in 1977.

In 1982, Rudi organised a Ganjifa demonstration show at the Vienna Museum of Ethnology. Rudi summoned Lora's three daughters Martina, Nandita and Anu to join in as actors. 'We wore sarees, sat on the floor. He scurried around and quickly showed us how these cards are played,' said Anu Chowdhury Sorabjee, the youngest of the three siblings.

Dr. Jyotindra Jain, an art historian and former director of the National Handloom and Handicrafts Museum, and the first dean of the School of Art and Aesthetics at Jawaharlal Nehru National University in New Delhi, met Rudi in the early 1980s in connection with his research on Ganjifa cards. 'Being married to an Austrian, and having studied in Vienna, we had a connection; we spoke with him in German,' Jyotindra Jain said. 'I was interested in popular culture and paint. Rudi, on the one hand, was interested in modern and contemporary art. He believed that even though India was riding the wave of modernism, the traditional arts and crafts were the country's greatest legacies.'

When Jyotindra Jain was working at the Shreyas Folk Museum in Ahmedabad, which opened in 1977, Rudi came to meet with him with his set of cards and to corroborate historical dates. 'I distinctly remember one thing—I told him to visit a Fort in Bhavnagar in Gujarat, in which there were extremely well-preserved paintings of local battles. These paintings were printed on playing cards and were brought out by the Maharaja of Bhavnagar. I showed the cards to Rudi. He got so excited that he asked me to get my hands on them. I went to locate the card box in Bhavnagar, but the shopkeeper hiked the price," he said.

Jyotindra Jain guided Rudi to explore places like Sawantwadi in Maharashtra and the Raja Dinkar Kelkar Museum in Pune. 'The Ganjifa cards were his great fascination,' noted Gulam Mohammed Sheikh, a painter and teacher based in Baroda at M.S. University. 'When he visited Baroda, he wanted to document some murals. He wanted to see some connection between the Ganjifa drawings and the traditional mural. I took him to the Kamnath Mahadev Temple located on the ghats of the Vishwamitri river.'

Constructed in the early nineteenth century, the temple features eight decorative idols, each positioned as if playing musical instruments. Rudi entered with his tripod and camera, eagerly capturing everything. 'While shooting, he started to talk about Ara, Husain, Schlesinger and shared about his time in the 1940s in the art world. We had a productive day,' said Sheikh, also an art historian and writer.

✣

Rudi felt a sense of familiarity around old monuments. Each time he was in Delhi, he paid homage to the tombs of Jamali and Kamali, located in the historic Mehrauli Archaeological Park. When he was on a Ganjifa research trip in India in 1982, a stay with the Khanna clan and a visit to the tombs of Jamali and Kamali were on his itinerary.

The tombs are remarkable examples of Indo-Islamic architecture, blending elements of the Lodhi and Mughal styles. Jamali, whose full name was Shaikh Fazlullah or Jalal Khan, was a renowned Sufi saint, mystic and poet who lived during the late fifteenth century. His spiritual teachings and poetry gained him a following among the local population, and he became a respected figure in the region.

Kamali's identity, on the other hand, remains unknown. Some historians suggest that he was a disciple of Jamali, while others speculate that he may have been a close companion or relative.

The tomb of Jamali, constructed from red sandstone, is a single-domed structure with an octagonal base—an architectural feature commonly associated with the Lodhi dynasty. The central dome is adorned with intricate calligraphy and geometric designs, showcasing the mastery of the craftsmen of that era. The arches and doorways are splendidly decorated with floral motifs and Quranic inscriptions. Inside the tomb, the central chamber houses the cenotaph of Jamali, while the walls are adorned with ornate stucco work.

Kamali's tomb, situated next to Jamali's, exhibits a striking resemblance to its counterpart. It is also an octagonal structure with a single dome, featuring the same red sandstone construction and intricate embellishments. However, Kamali's tomb differs in one major aspect—its interior. The interior of Kamali's tomb is decorated with blue and yellow glazed tiles. Inside this tomb, the central chamber contains two cenotaphs, believed to be those of Kamali and an unidentified individual. The identity of the second occupant remains a mystery, adding to the intrigue.

What sets these tombs apart is the enigmatic atmosphere that surrounds them. Local folklore and urban legends speak of strange occurrences at the site, such as unexplained sounds and ghostly apparitions. 'On that particular visit, Rudi shared that when he went there with Nena, many years ago, she felt the energy was off; she was very sensitive. And then he said something to me that left me feeling a bit unsettled,' Krishen Khanna said, in a sombre tone.

While he walked out of the gates of the historical site, Rudi turned and said: 'Khanna, I don't know if I'll ever return here again.'

AFTERWORD: THE TREE FALLS

Upon his return to a snowy Vienna, on 22 February 1983, Rudi wrote to Krishen Khanna a long-handwritten letter, discussing his 'peaceful week in Pune with the Khandalavalas.' He had several articles soon-to-be-published. Rudi complained about contracting influenza and suffering from an unrelenting cough. The medicines made him tired, and he had 'so much to do and write!'

He thought back 'with love, gratitude, and happiness to my life with my family in Delhi and in Shimla. I feel so much at home with all of you … I feel quite lost here, alone and deserted.'[92]

He was looking forward to hosting Malti and her husband Shekhar Shah, who were travelling from the US to Europe and stopping over in Vienna.

'Uncle Rudi, I am coming to Vienna,' Malti beamed over a telephone call.

'Rakshasa! Looking forward to seeing you,' Rudi exclaimed.

'I hope it's alright for the Rakshasa's husband to join in,' Malti laughed.

'Yes, of course.'

The meeting never happened.

Rudi passed away two days after that call on 25 March 1983.

The news arrived as a shock to Marie-Louise, as it did to everybody who knew him. 'Biba (Rudi's sister Victoria) called me and informed me about Rudi's passing. Biba was close to him. I collapsed when I heard the news. And on my mother's insistence, I left for Vienna,' shared Marie-Louise.

Rudi came to India ahead of
the Second World War

Before his passing, Rudi was immersed in writing the final chapter of his book on Ganjifa cards. He worked in a beautiful location near the Schönbrunn Palace, surrounded by the captivating scenery. There, he would often be found at his desk, deeply engrossed on his typewriter. 'I don't know what happened. But from what we as a family understood, he felt so unwell that he went to the door of his flat, opened it, gave out a loud cry, and fell down.' [93]

The sudden thud prompted the neighbour's terrier to bark, which quickly alerted the fellow residents. They immediately called for a rescue car. But it was too late.

In an emotional tribute to Rudi, Krishen Khanna expressed his deep concern and affection for his old friend:

> Seeing you leading this somewhat solitary existence, I asked you what would happen if you took ill. You guessed what was on my mind and pointed to the neighbours next door. "They look in frequently", you said. Yet when the Angel announced his entry, there

was no one. You had realised as much. With your usual efficiency and eye to detail, you made the Angel wait, called up the medical emergency, donned on your greatcoat, your muffler, your fur cap, your gloves, kept the door open and sat down beside the telephone and waited. That's where they found you, all ready for your journey. They tried but couldn't bring you back.

Someone called me the next morning, I think it was Lolly and I felt the last lines of *The Exile's Letter* which you so loved:

"And if you ask how I regret that parting

It was like the flowers falling at Spring's end

Confused, whirled in a tangle."

And now the things and people you so loved are scattered and you rest with your ancestors in Partenkirchen.

Au revoir dear friend, may we recognise each other, even in our different shapes, in our future lives and continue where we had left.[94]

✣

Albrecht delivered the eulogy at his brother's funeral, being arguably the most appropriate family member to speak on Rudi's legacy. The brothers had spent thirty-four years together in a close-knit community. During the service, a piece by Antonín Leopold Dvorák, Rudi's favorite Czech composer, was played. Rudi was laid to rest at the Friedhof Partenkirchen cemetery, alongside the graves of his parents and brother Ernst. 'A life without Rudi will

Rudi with Shiavax Chavda (L) and George Keyt (middle)

be a different life for us,' Albrecht said. 'We must try to adapt to him and live in deep gratitude from what Rudi has left us, a rich, beautiful and wonderful memory of a fulfilling life.'

Life, according to Rudi, was in the doing.

A young German geologist, arriving in India under unexpected circumstances, quickly shifts his career path and discovers his true passion in art. He then transitions to a dynamic corporate role, eventually emerging as a prominent expert on ancient Indian playing cards.

Rudi's legacy has stood the test of time through the lives he managed to touch and the artistic careers he helped to shape. Perhaps the most fitting summary of Rudi's life journey can be found in his own words.

In a 1980 letter addressed to Krishen Khanna, Rudi shared: 'My days as an art critic of *The Times* were really the most important for me in all my life in India. Not only because of the friendships I made which lasted a lifetime, but because I had to come to terms with myself, in my attitudes and opinions and in my endeavour to "cut out the cackle". When words begin to count,

Rudi purchased this set of Ganjifa cards in 1977

not in numbers and in great sound, but in meaning, then you know you have got somewhere.'[95]

After his passing, a remembrance meeting was held at the Artists' Centre, led by his close friend Ara, who, poignantly, passed away exactly two years after Rudi. The gathering saw attendance not just from the art community, but also members of the Advertising Club and Voltas, all paying rich tributes. Rudi had visited India in January that year, and many found it hard to believe he was no longer there. Karl Khandalavala also spoke, reflecting on his forty-year association with Rudi and their travels to various temples in India. Lolly received condolence letters from Khorshed and Kekoo Gandhy, sharing Karl Khandalavala's reminiscences as well as from Raza and Mulk Raj. However, the loss was felt most personally by two artists, Ara and Krishen Khanna.

Lucy was acutely aware of the significance of Krishen Khanna's friendship to Rudi. In a deeply-felt note to Krishen Khanna, she expressed a range of emotions—her observations, regrets and the apprehension of impending loneliness. Rudi and Lucy had once considered beginning a new life together, but fate had a different plan. She marvelled at the tributes Rudi received—he was to be presented with the 'Cross of Honour' by the Austrian Government—and said something which struck both Krishen Khanna and James: 'Rudi lived and died like a tree ...'

Almost four decades after since Rudi's passing, in April 2018, James found himself sorting through stacks of documents in his studio in Lewes, East Sussex. In that moment, he took a pause to contemplate the possible meaning behind Lucy's words.

'Aside from being tall and strong like a tree, he put down deep roots wherever he went. He wasn't a slight person in any way. He also sheltered people. He looked after the artists without expecting anything in return. And after standing tall for so many years, one day he just fell...' [96]

✣

I do believe that there has been some divine synchronicity at play since this subject found me. The extraordinary epiphanic moments that unfolded over the past seven years are a testimony.

It all started with a chance encounter with Krishen Khanna in 2016. He wondered what *The Times* was doing with the writings of his close friend, Rudolf von Leyden. This meeting set the wheels in motion for the creation of this book, and it's just one of many fortuitous moments that would shape the years ahead.

I had met Krishen Khanna in connection with a tribute to his late artist friend Raza, whose foundation ended up being one of the key supporters of the book. This reaffirmed my belief in the serendipity of this project.

I began by mining through *The Times* archives. The wealth of historical material I uncovered was riveting. Originally, I intended to compile Rudi's art writings, which ranged from 1938 to the 1940s and sporadically from the 1950s to the 1960s. However, the scope of his work was so vast and illuminating that it compelled me, along with the support of Dadiba Pundole, to extend the book's coverage to encompass art writings up to the end of the century, going beyond mere reviews. This long, arduous task led to the making of another book tracing 150 years of art writings in *The Times of India.*

While that project oscillated between exhilarating discoveries and mind-numbingly mundane tasks, I simultaneously scoured the vast expanse of Google to learn more about Rudi. My search yielded only a handful of articles and mentions.

Then, in 2017, a casual Google search led me to James von Leyden, author of two crime thrillers set in Morocco, *A Death in the Medina* and *Last Boat from Tangier*. I reached out to him through LinkedIn, enquiring whether he was related to Rudolf von Leyden. A little shy of a month later, he responded, confirming that he was indeed Rudi's nephew.

He encouraged me to apply for a grant and visit Lewes in East Sussex, where he resides. 'If you're genuinely committed to this project,' he said, '...you're welcome to stay and explore the contents in my studio.'

Meeting James marked a pivotal moment in my research. He connected me with his cousin Flora Veit-Wild, who introduced me to Rudi's third partner, Udi-Jutta Schneewind, both based in Berlin. Flora also facilitated my meeting with Marie-Louise von Leyden, their oldest cousin residing in Bonn.

Unsure of the journey that lay ahead, I embarked on a trip to Europe and the UK in April 2018, thanks to the generous support of art patron Priyasri Patodia and the Bodhana Arts and Research Foundation. Little did I know that this trip would ultimately culminate in the creation of this book.

My first stop was Paris. James suggested I meet with Gwenael Beuchet, Attaché de Conservation du Patrimoine at the Musée Français de la Carte à Jouer. Gwenael had extensively researched Rudi's involvement with Ganjifa playing cards and shared numerous articles with me. Rudi's passion for Mughul and Dasavatara Ganjifa cards prompted him to sell a substantial portion of his collection to the Deutsches Spielkartenmuseum, the German Playing Card Museum, in Leinfelden-Echterdingen in 1972. During my visit, I had the opportunity to explore this collection, which consisted of 900 individual cards, as well as a diverse range of historical Indian playing cards.

My next destination was Bonn, a city along the Rhine river, adorned with cherry blossom trees in April. Marie-Louise von Leyden warmly welcomed me to her apartment, away from the main city centre. A painting of a landscape was perched at the entrance. 'Do you know Paleeee Hill in Bombay?' she asked, pointing to the painting, 'That little path leads you to the beach front.'

'You see that little pathway,' I told her, '...that's where I grew up—on Sherly Rajan Road. I spent most of my teenage years walking up and down the slope.'

Now a prime real estate address, Pali Hill was once a sylvan haven where farmhouses and sprawling bungalows nestled.

Marie-Louise spoke animatedly as we shared a meal over a couple of hours at her favourite restaurant, overlooking the Rhine river.

The trip continued with a meeting in Berlin with Udi. She was, and is, by her own admission, a deeply complex woman.

Flora had a keen interest in the 'old Bombay.' Together, we delved into Rudi's most challenging-to-decipher handwritten letters, notes, photographs and the wealth of materials that bring joy to a researcher. Flora graciously assisted by translating many of the letters exchanged within the family, originally written in German, helping me piece together various aspects of Rudi's life story.

Then, there was James' attic in East Sussex, a veritable treasure trove of aging letters, photographs, diary entries, newspaper clippings, magazine articles, documents and artworks. I meticulously photographed nearly everything in that room.

The access to the record of these lives—letters, essays and diary notes—inform the bulk of this research.

In between my time in Germany and the UK, I stopped over in Vienna. I met with Dr. Christian Schicklgruber, the deputy director of the Weltmuseum Wien, where Rudi donated a part of his Ganjifa card collection and his enviable Indian antiques.

On that trip, I even met with the feisty Eleonore Chowdhury-Haberl. If history has to classify the late Billy Chowdhury and her as Bombay's first art collector couple, it wouldn't be entirely off the mark.

Back in India, I reached out to people who had a connection to the Bombay that Rudi knew so well. Advertisers and theatre veterans Gerson da Cunha and Alyque Padamsee, along with Mithoo Coorlawalla, shared their insights. Mithoo knew Rudi's first wife Nena, Alyque recounted Rudi's encouragement to explore beyond Tennessee Williams, and da Cunha spoke about his open yet authoritative nature.

It was almost poetic when da Cunha spoke about Rudi and revisited memories of old Bombay at his spacious flat in an Art Deco building, located along the western edge of the Oval Maidan, facing the imposing Victorian Gothic buildings. It felt like the present echoing the past.

Da Cunha introduced me to Los Angeles-based Shanmil Herzog, who shared invaluable stories about Rudi's second wife, Lucy Del Marle-Blake, and their relationship.

Artists Nalini Malani and Gieve Patel recalled how Rudi's opinions about their work gave much-needed impetus to their nascent practices. 'He was already a well-known figure in Bombay. I had just finished my medical school. I was flattered that he should have noticed me,' Gieve said of Rudi's encouragement.

The one artist that he truly rooted for was K.H. Ara. Practically every story relating to Rudi mentioned Ara. The patronage of Ara by Cowasji and Hirji Jehangir was a known fact in art circles, but hearing it from Jehangir Jehangir and Adi Jehangir, his sons, and trustees of the Jehangir Art Gallery, brought in a fresh perspective.

In between my discussion with Adi, he casually asked me, 'Who worked with Voltas? Leyden or Langhammer?'

'Leyden!' came my reply.

'Then you must meet my good friend Katy Soonawalla,' he insisted.

Rudi held a high-ranking position as the publicity and marketing director at Voltas for over two decades. However, apart from the notes I received from his family, I had no other leads. Meeting Katy, Rudi's former secretary at Voltas, helped connect the dots.

Katy was warm, open, and still in deep admiration of her first and only boss, 'one of the kindest men' she had the privilege of knowing. The fact that her daughter-in-law, graphic designer Ayesha Soonawalla—whom I fortuitously met at a lecture at Pundoles' five years after meeting Katy—would design the cover of this volume is another uncanny happenstance that astonishes me.

In Delhi, two illustrious art historians, Geeta Kapur and Yashodhara Dalmia, highlighted why Rudi's role as an art critic was catalytic, not only in the insightful criticism he provided but also in laying down the parameters for reviewing and assessing Indian art. At that meeting, Kapur urged me to meet with painter, art historian and writer Gulam Mohammed Sheikh in Baroda. During Rudi's visit to Baroda, he handed over a precious leather-bound scrapbook to Sheikh, in the hope it would someday find its way into a suitable archive. Back then, Rudi couldn't think of anyone better to look after it than Sheikh, who taught art history and painting for nearly three decades at the Faculty of Fine Arts, M.S. University, Baroda.

Since his retirement, the original scrapbook comprising several newspaper clippings, personal notes, art observations and pictures sits at his studio in Baroda, where I had the pleasure of perusing it. The material from the scrapbook has been digitised by the Asia Art Archive (AAA).

In addition to the AAA, the ever-efficient teams at *The Times of India* (TOI), The Raza Foundation (TRF), Tata Central Archives (TCA), Chhatrapati Shivaji Maharaj Vastu Sangrahalaya (CSMVS) as well as Chemould Archives provided me with indispensable material that can be found referenced in the book.

Each archive provided a unique perspective on Rudi's life and work. TRF helped me with several personal letters exchanged between the art critic and Raza. Meanwhile, old issues of Voltas' *WE* magazine and correspondence from TCA oriented me into Rudi's corporate life, while the frayed images carefully restored by Chemould provided a snapshot into that era.

Despite making progress, I only managed to write two chapters before setting the unfinished manuscript aside. Fortunately, I had the privilege of reconnecting with Dr. Pheroza Godrej. She had known Rudi and Nena as friends of her parents. Over the last seven years, she has been a constant source of guidance and support whenever the research became daunting or faced roadblocks. She emphasised that this book must see its logical conclusion, motivating me to return to the manuscript.

In 2020, Covid-19 changed life across the globe. I initially thought I would complete the book. However, I ended up spending my time learning traditional Indian art online. The experience moved me deeply, and I yearned to learn more. Three individuals directed me to Anu Chowdhury Sorabjee, a patron of traditional art for the last three decades. Upon meeting her, I discovered that she was Eleonore Chowdhury-Haberl's third daughter. We had meaningful discussions about her mother, and naturally, Rudi became a prominent topic of conversation.

That day, I went back to my folders and dug out a picture I had taken of Anu's mother when we met at her apartment in Vienna. She was seated alongside her favourite Gaitonde painting. Remorse set in as I went through all the folders, wondering when this story would find a home. I returned to the dossier every now and then, piecing together a life that seemed so familiar yet distant from me.

Three years later, I was invited to speak about my research at the Austro-Indian Association in Vienna, where Rudi had served as president for two terms. I debated whether to visit Garmisch-Partenkirchen during this trip, where the family's old home and Rudi's grave are located. I pondered whether this would add anything to my research.

It was Anu who encouraged me to embark on this quest and pay my respects at Rudi's grave. 'You are writing his biography; how can you not go and seek his blessings?' she asked.

In that moment, I knew I had to pray at his grave. I don't quite know why, but visiting his resting place, surrounded by the Alps in the Bavarian town, made Rudi seem hauntingly real.

From that moment on, Rudi's presence transcended the distant, mythical character I was researching and writing about.

And in a stroke of divine synchronicity, this biography found its publisher just a fortnight later.

Dear Speaking Tiger Books, thank you for becoming the right home for The Catalyst, Rudolf von Leyden...

The Critic, portrait of Rudi, by Walter Langhammer

courtesy of Tata Institute of Fundamental Research

ACKNOWLEDGEMENTS

To Rudolf von Leyden's family—Flora Veit-Wild, James von Leyden, Lucie Velterop von Leyden and Marie-Louise von Leyden—thank you for your big heartedness, trust, support and patience.

To Krishen Khanna and his family—Karan, Malti, Rasika and Renu—thank you for being the spark that ignited this journey and being an indispensable part of it.

To all the interviewees, my humble gratitude. I have thoroughly enjoyed the oral histories. Thank you for your time and openness.

To Jesal Thacker and Priyasri Patodia, thank you for believing in the project from the get-go!

To Achim Fabig and the German Federal Foreign Office, thank you for helping the book see the light of day.

To Ashok Vajpeyi and The Raza Foundation, thank you for recognising the book's potential.

To Manjiri Latey, thank you for making me realise the book first in my mind's eye and then in reality.

To Meenal Baghel, thank you for your unwavering encouragement and helping me stay on track.

To Meru Gokhale, thank you for your incredible insight, direction and for steadying the ship.

To Diya Isha, thank you for your diligence and for the hours you've poured over this manuscript.

To Ayesha Soonawalla, thank you for the most-fitting tribute cover and for your infectious enthusiasm.

To Rishita Chandra, thank you for giving this book a wonderful visual semblance.

To Bharati Khule, thank you for your immense patience and hard work towards putting this book together.

To Renuka Chatterjee, thank you for hand holding me through the daunting publishing process.

To Dr. Pheroza Godrej, thank you for the faith that you have shown in my work and for being the guiding light of this book.

To Bernhard Steinruecke, thank you for being the wheels that drove this project forward in every way.

To the silent supporters of the book—Aadya Jajodia, Ananya Bhatia, Anjana Vaswani, Anil Bhatti, Anu Chowdhury Sorabjee, Dadiba Pundole, Gurvinderjit Samra, Harshada Mane, Jayant Balan, Jonas Stolze, Michael Pal, Purnima Thacker, P.C. Johnson, Rajendra Prasad Narla, Roshini Vadehra, Sabyasachi Mukherjee, Sharon Elisabeth, Shilpa Gupta, Shireen Gandhy, Shreevatsa Nevatia, Vijay Darji and Tanika Thacker—you have all impacted this book in your own way. Thank you!

To my family and friends, thank you for your understanding and encouragement.

To my husband Sameer Desai, thank you for being my anchor and to Alo, for being my greatest cheer leader.

And to the divine hand that guided this project, reaffirming my belief that there are no coincidences.

‘Thank you for helping us see ourselves…’

When Rudi left India in 1968,
the artist community
got together and presented him
with their self-portraits.

A. A. Almelkar

Sultan Ali

K. H. Ara

Prabhakar Barwe

Bal Chhabda

V. S. Gaitonde

Satish Gujral

Prafulla Joshi

Janine Mongillat

Farokh Mulla

Laxman Pai

Satish Panchal

Naren Panchal

Homi Patel

Pilloo Pochkhanwalla

Badri Narayan

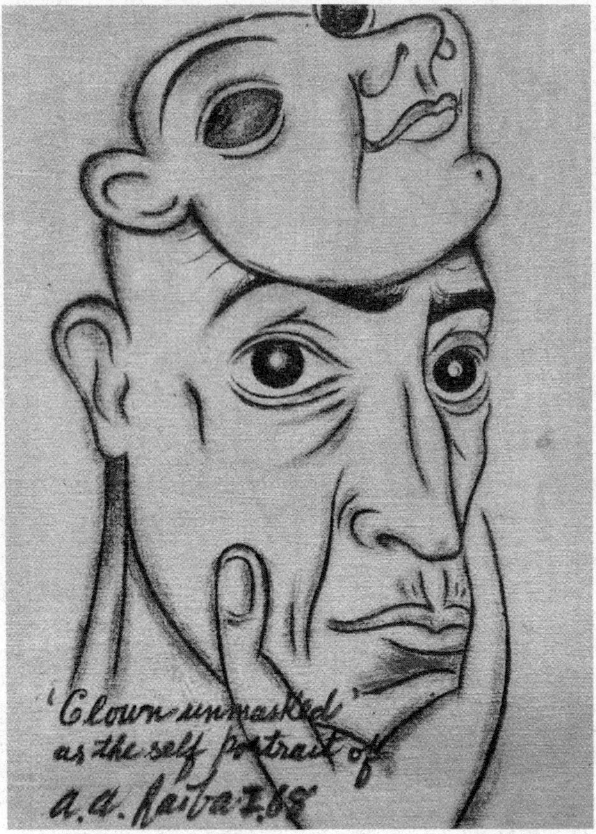

A. A. Raiba

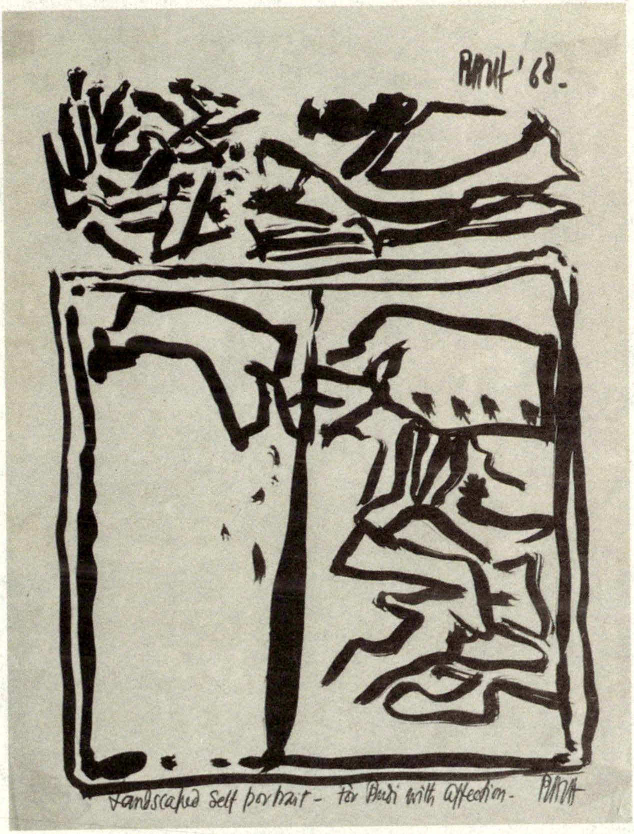

S. H. Raza

Akbar Padamsee

P. T. Reddy

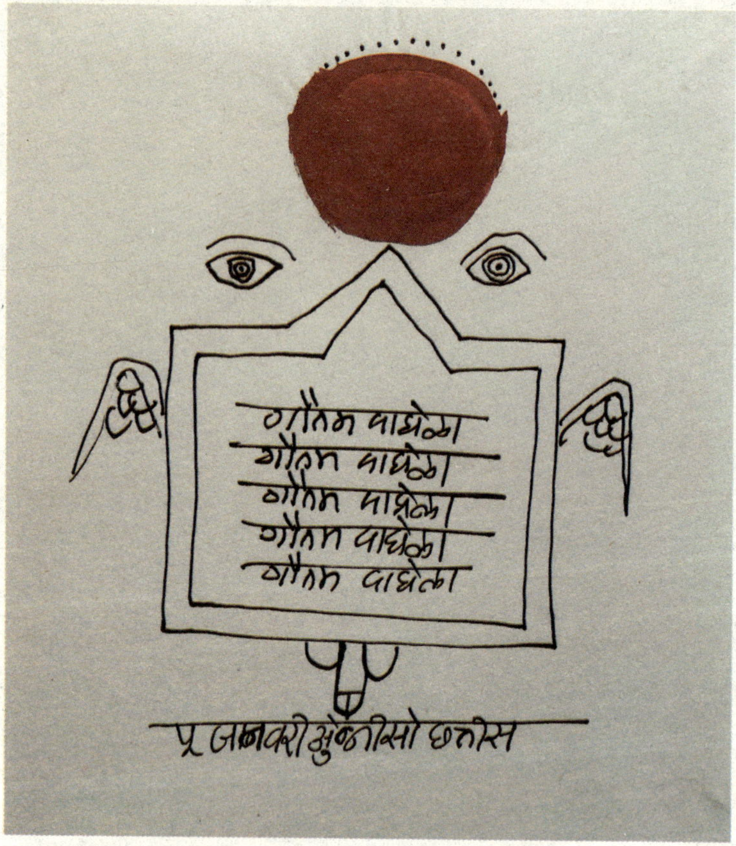

Gautam Vaghela

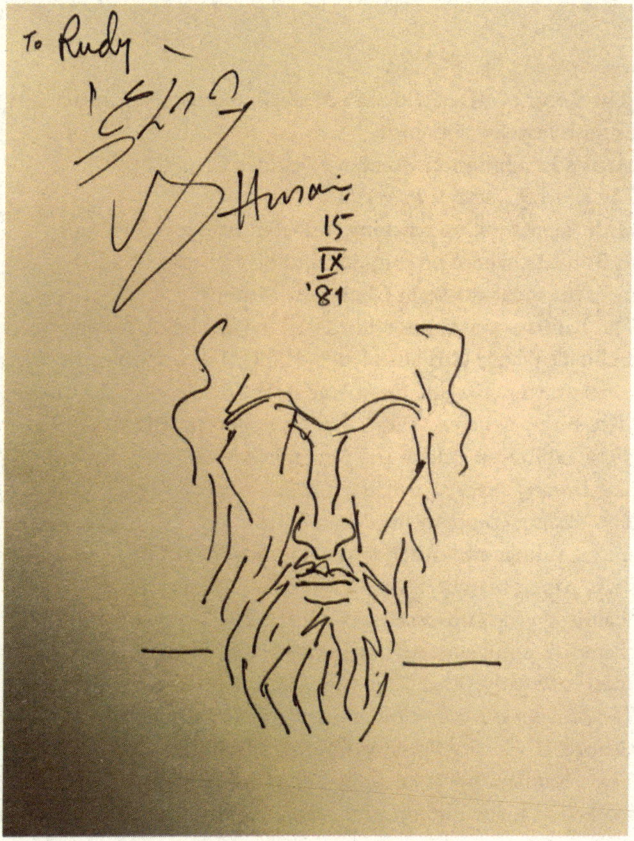

M. F. Husain

ENDNOTES

1 'The Return of Desdemona'; *Mumbai Mirror*; 25 January 2014
2 English novelist and critic
3 'Artists Exhibition in Bombay: Distinct Group';
The Times of India; 9 July 1949
4 Gade, later took up teaching in Delhi, before returning
to Bombay, where he painted until his last days in 2001
from his small studio in Chembur, Mumbai
5 The Bauhaus was founded in 1919 in the city of Weimar by German
architect Walter Gropius (1883–1969). Its core objective was a radical
concept: to reimagine the material world to reflect the unity of all the arts
6 'The Bombayman's Diary'; *The Evening New*; 30 April 1954
7 'First exhibition held at the Jehangir Art Gallery';
The Times of India; 1 February 1952
8 The trading company imported cotton, tea, oil, coffee, cocoa,
spices, rubber and other colonial goods from India and exported
soap, paper, matches, watches, textiles and machinery
9 'Painting is not obscene, says court'; *The Times of India*; 17 June 1954
10 'Painting is not obscene, says court'; *The Times of India*; 17 June 1954
11 Interview with Akbar Padamsee; Mumbai; 17 May 2017
12 *The Making of Modern Indian Art: The Progressives*;
Oxford University Press; Yashodhara Dalmia
13 Vivan Sundaram was an Indian contemporary artist. He
worked in many different medias, including painting, sculpture,
printmaking, photography, installation, and video art, and his
work was politically conscious and highly intertextual in nature
14 'Art in India in not commercialised'; *The Times of
India*; Dnyaneshwar Nadkarni; 3 March 1982
15 Piero della Francesca was an Italian painter of the Early
Renaissance. His painting is characterised by its serene
humanism, its use of geometric forms and perspective
16 'Citylights', *The Times of India*, 2003

17 Exhibition notes from the NS Documentation Centre, Munich; 11 August 2023

18 *Growing Up Under the Weimar Republic, 1918-1933: Reflections on Personal Identity and the Past;* Wolfgang von Leyden

19 Two race-based measures depriving Jews of rights, designed by Adolf Hitler and approved by the Nazi Party at a convention in Nuremberg on 15 September 1935

20 Interview with Udi-Jutta Schneewind; Berlin; 18 April 2018
Interview with James von Leyden; East Sussex; 23-25 April 2018

21 Marie-Louise von Leyden recalled an incident she often discussed with her uncle. In 1930, the year she was born, Rudi's life was in great danger. He was in Greece working on his thesis on the 'Aspects of Vulcanism in Gulf of Aegina.' 'He was pursuing his doctorate when he contracted typhus. My grandparents received a letter. My grandmother left for Athens immediately,' she said.

22 'Art Notes and Events'; *The Bombay Chronicle*; Kanaiyalal Vakil; 17 May 1936

23 *Citizen Gallery*; Speaking Tiger Books; Jerry pinto

24 'Rest of Bombay Beaten in Women's Charity Hockey Match'; *The Times of India*; 8 March 1935

25 Interview with Dr Hemant Morparia; Mumbai; October 2018

26 Walter Langhammer; askART website

27 *Citizen Gallery*; Speaking Tiger Books; Jerry pinto

28 *The Making of Modern Indian Art: The Progressives*; Oxford University Press; Yashodhara Dalmia

29 *Citizen Gallery*; Speaking Tiger Books; Jerry pinto

30 Research material by Dr. Margit Franz, 2007

31 'Luise von Leyden as a chronicler of Jewish exile in India'; essay by Flora Veit-Wild

32 *Mumbai Fables*; Princeton University Press; Gyan Prakash

33 Currently known as Dr. Bhulabhai Desai Road

34 'Ye Olde Sweatshop'; essay by Rudolf von Leyden; Vienna 1979

35 'Ye Olde Sweatshop'; essay by Rudolf von Leyden; Vienna 1979

36 'Art in Independent India'; *The Times of India*; R.v. Leyden; 15 August 1949

37 Opening speech by Rudolf von Leyden for S.H. Raza's Exhibition; 1949

38 Both Marie-Louise von Leyden and Eleonore Chowdhury-Haberl recounted the same story in their interviews in 2018

39 *The Making of Modern India Art:* The Progressives; Oxford University Press; Yashodhara Dalmia

40 'Ara was more than a father'; *Mumbai Mirror*; Reema Gehi; 14 April 2019

41 'Ara'; R.v. Leyden; courtesy of Rudi's scrapbook; Gulam Mohammad Sheikh; Asia Art Archive

42 'Ara'; R.v. Leyden; courtesy of Rudi's scrapbook; Gulam Mohammad Sheikh; Asia Art Archive
43 'Exhibition of Paintings: The Self-Taught Artist'; *The Times of India*; 30 December 1942
44 'Ara'; R.v. Leyden; Lalit Kala Akademi, Delhi
45 Essay on Artists' Centre; Madhusudan Kumar; 2020
46 Interview with Madhusudan Kumar; Artists' Centre, Mumbai; August 2018
47 'Ara'; R.v. Leyden; Lalit Kala Akademi, Delhi
48 'Artists' Exhibition in Bombay: Distinct Group'; *The Times of India*; 9 July 1949
49 'Ara'; R.v. Leyden; Lalit Kala Akademi, Delhi
50 Interview with Nalini Malani; Mumbai; August 2020
51 Interview with Adi Jehangir; Mumbai; June 2018
52 Emanuel Schlesinger; Private Archive Dr. Margit Franz, Sinabelkirchen
53 *The Making of Modern Indian Art: The Progressives*; Oxford University Press; Yashodhara Dalmia
54 *The Making of Modern Indian Art: The Progressives*; Oxford University Press; Yashodhara Dalmia
55 *The Making of Modern Indian Art: The Progressives*; Oxford University Press; Yashodhara Dalmia
56 'Sparkling Colours'; *The Times of India;* R.v.L; 17 January 1948
57 'Exhibition of Paintings: tributes Paid to Artists'; *The Times of India*; 11 December 1954
58 *Citizen Gallery*; Speaking Tiger Books; Jerry Pinto
59 'Professor Langhammer "Sincere Friend of the Art World" Farewell Party'; *The Times of India*; 5 April 1957
60 *The Making of Modern Indian Art: The Progressives*; Oxford University Press; Yashodhara Dalmia
61 Interview with Marie-Louise von Leyden; Bonn; April 2018
62 'Rudi von Leyden'; *WE*; 1967 (courtesy: Tata Central Archives)
63 'Indian Sculpture: An Exhibition of 50 Photographs'; Rudi von Leyden; 1947
64 *WE*; 1968
65 'Nena Memorial Exhibition: Sensitive Painters'; *The Times of India*; 30 August 1966
66 'Art exhibition'; *The Times of India*; 8 September 1950
67 *WE*; Rudi von Leyden; 1967
68 'Anand Adventure'; Rudi von Leyden; July 1982
69 Interview with Katy Soonawalla; Mumbai; June 2018
70 'Dr. Homi Bhabha and the World of Art'; R. v. Leyden; 1966
71 Excerpt from F.N. Souza's autobiographical essay, *'Nirvana of A Maggot'*
72 'Artists in the New Republic'; *The Times of India*; Rudi von Leyden; 26 January 1950

73 Alyque Padamsee was the chief executive at Lintas for many years; he created iconic ads like Surf's Lalitaji, Hamara Bajaj and Liril girl. In his advertising career, he built over 100 brands and advertising characters such as Cherry Charlie for Cherry Blossom Shoe Polish, MRF Muscle Man and the Kamasutra couple. He also created many public service campaigns on topics, including eve-teasing, AIDS and sexual molestation

74 Interview with Alyque Padamsee; Mumbai; June 2018

75 *The Making of Modern Art: The Progressives*; Oxford University Press; Yashodhara Dalmia

76 'Lull in European Art: Modern Painters Disappoint', *The Times of India*, 25 September 1953

77 Interview with Marie-Louise von Leyden; Bonn; April 201

78 Letter addressed to S.H. Raza and Janine; 1964

79 Excerpt from a letter by Rudolf von Leyden to S.H. Raza and Janine; 1964

80 'Exhibition of Paintings: 400 Pictures on View'; *The Times of India*; 15 November 1949

81 N.S. Bendre painted landscapes and portraits, rendered in different stylistic idioms

82 Opening speech by Rudolf von Leyden for S.H. Raza's exhibition; 1949; courtesy of Rudi's scrapbook; Gulam Mohammad Sheikh; Asia Art Archive

83 Essay for a catalogue; R.von Leyden; 1959

84 Essay for a catalogue; R.von Leyden; 1959

85 'The Bindu of Life Ends'; *Mumbai Mirror*; Dr. Saryu Doshi; 24 July 2016

86 Excerpt from a letter by Rudolf von Leyden to S.H. Raza and Janine; 5 March 1966

87 'A Glimpse Into the Past'; *The Times of India*; 30 January 1968

88 'Ye Olde Sweatshop'; Rudi von Leyden; Vienna; 1979

89 Letter to Krishen and Renu Khanna; 2 February 1974

90 Essay; Rudi von Leyden; 8 January 1978

91 'Rudolf von Leyden'; exhibition catalogue; Goethe-Institut; 1999

92 Letter to Krishen Khanna; 22 February 1983

93 Interview with Marie-Louise von Leyden; Bonn; April 2018

94 Excerpt from, 'To Rudolf von Leyden: A Letter Out of Season', Krishen Khanna

95 Letter to Krishen Khanna; 31 August 1980

96 Interview with James von Leyden; East Sussex; April 2018

INDEX